Supporting the Literacy Needs of Children in the Early Years

by
Dorothy Smith

QEd

A QEd Publication

Published in 2001

© Dorothy Smith

ISBN 1 898873 22 4

British Library Cataloguing
A catalogue record for this book is available from the British Library.

Published by QEd, The ROM Building, Eastern Avenue,
Lichfield, Staffs. WS13 6RN
Web site: www.qed.uk.com
Email: orders@qed.uk.com

Printed in the United Kingdom by Stowes (Stoke-on-Trent).

Contents

Chapter 1
Language and literacy within the curriculum

Literacy links the four skills of reading, writing, speaking and listening. It crosses curriculum boundaries and is at the heart of education. The process of becoming literate begins in the home and continues even when learners have left school and further education establishments. It is set centrally within Government documents pertaining to the foundation stage and those concerned with school Key Stages.

The foundation stage of education includes children from the age of three to the end of their Reception Year. It is a preparation for working within Key Stage 1. Because of the importance of early years education, help for those educators has been given in *Curriculum guidance for the foundation stage* (QCA, 2000). This is intended to help those adults who work in the foundation stage to plan and teach an appropriate curriculum. It details what are termed 'stepping stones' which indicate the knowledge, skills, understanding and attitudes that children should learn in order to achieve the designated early learning goals.

Part of the early years curriculum is 'communication, language and literacy'. Where listening skills are concerned there is a section on attention skills and persistence which will link with the section on listening and attention in this book on pages 9 and 10. Receptive language is mentioned where children should be given the chance to listen carefully. Expressive language is dealt with under the heading 'language and communication' where children should be given opportunities to talk and communicate in a wide range of situations, to respond to others and to practise and enlarge the scope of their vocabulary and oral language skills. Early skills of reading and writing should be built up through experiencing a wide range of books and for learning about words through exploration and enjoyment. The guidance stresses the importance of language skills by stating:

'The development and use of communication and language is at the heart of young children's learning.' (page 45)

The National Curriculum Handbook for Primary Teachers in England Key Stages 1 and 2 (QCA, 1999) sets out six key skills areas to be covered within primary education. Communication is one of these and the areas of speaking, listening, reading and writing are included under this heading. It is emphasised that these four areas are not separate and therefore:

> 'Teaching should ensure that work in speaking and listening, reading and writing is integrated.' (page 44)

There is a distinction between the terms 'language', 'communication' and 'literacy' although often these seem to be used interchangeably. Communication is the sending of messages from the transmitter to the receiver. This can be between two individuals or from one person to many. These messages can be spoken, can be given through non-verbal means, can be written and can be read. Understanding of these messages is required in order for communication to be successful.

Language is used by individuals in order to help better communication. Again this can be spoken or written and it requires knowledge of words, concepts and sentences. Language is a well-established formalised system and when written is symbolic, using set marks or characters. Literacy as already mentioned requires the individual to be able to read and write with competence and, in order for that to occur, proficiency in language and communication (speaking and listening) is most necessary.

In 1996 the DfEE set up the *National Literacy Project* which became the *National Literacy Strategy*. This was to help counteract the problems some children encounter in reading and writing when they transfer from Key Stage 2 to Key Stage 3, from the primary to the secondary sector. As David Blunkett, the Secretary of State for Education and Employment at that time, stated in his foreword:

> 'All our children deserve to leave school equipped to enter a fulfilling adult life. But if children do not master the basic skills of literacy ... while they are at primary school, they will be seriously disadvantaged later.'

The Government set literacy targets for 11 year-olds and produced a comprehensive document which specified various detailed objectives for reading and writing which would be followed each term. This also set out how one hour per day could be structured in order to meet the targets. The Literacy Hour starts in the Reception year and because of the staged entry of children into these Reception classes the objectives are set for the whole Reception year rather than termly as in the subsequent years, and it is advised that there should be a great deal of repetition and consolidation. It is also realised that some Reception-aged children are placed within Year 1 classes and that some are summer entrants with only one term of formal schooling so this 'overlearning' might need to be carried forward into Year 1.

Although the Framework does not set out separate speaking and listening objectives, these areas of the language curriculum are implicit within the teaching of reading and writing skills. This is recognised in the paragraph of the introduction that defines literacy:

'Good oral work enhances pupils' understanding of language in both oral and written forms and of the way language can be used to communicate. It is also an important part of the process through which pupils read and compose texts.'

Because of the need to teach speaking and listening skills, the Qualifications and Curriculum Authority (QCA) brought out a booklet entitled *Teaching speaking and listening in Key stages 1 and 2* (1999) which is intended to link with the literacy strategy and to give a framework guidance to teachers about teaching and assessing spoken language activities. It builds on what children bring to school and it recognises that early years settings and the home can help to provide children with a basis for language. It states that:

'Most children come into school with some ability to hold a conversation, persuade, argue and entertain others.' (page 3)

It does not present general teaching objectives or teaching ideas for children in the Reception class as it starts with Year 1. However, there are ideas that can be easily adapted for these younger children.

In the activity sections of this book, any ideas from the above documents will be incorporated alongside other suggestions.

Although the four strands of listening, speaking, reading and writing should not be taught as discrete units, for the ease of accessing this book each will be dealt with in turn. There are two chapters on each. One will describe the skill and how children acquire it. Links between the strands will also be discussed. The other chapter will examine some assessment techniques and provide activities and approaches to enhance learning. An additional chapter will discuss how effective language and literacy teaching and learning can take place within early years settings.

Chapter 2
Listening and the acquisition of received language

Sounds and words surround us from birth and even pre-birth. From the moment children are born they hear speech and over the years they become more adept at differentiating what they hear and making sense of the sounds. They learn the difference between music with words, and music without words. They realise that there are loud and soft sounds. They work out that animals make different sounds from people and that the latter produce words that have meanings. Listening is fundamental to the other aspects of language. It is an essential part of daily life within the home, the play situation and the learning setting. If there are problems with listening then understanding can be affected as can the production and use of oral language. Listening can be influenced by how one hears, how one understands and how motivated one is.

Attention control

Studies in early childhood development such as those described in *Helping Language Development* by Cooper, Moodley and Reynell (1978) conclude that listening develops through developmental stages. Although children do not always learn at the same rate, there are stages of attention control which appear to occur at different ages.

Before children reach three years old they show signs of extreme distractibility and their attention is held only momentarily by whatever becomes the dominant stimulus. The first signs of fixed attention are seen when children start to be able to concentrate for some time on a task of their own choice but they cannot cope with any adult intervention that might distract them. Around the age of three, children's attention is still single-channelled but this becomes more flexible. With an adult's help children can focus their attention and transfer from their own task to something under an adult's direction and then they can return to their original task. By the age of about four, children are usually still seen to be single-channelled. They must give their full auditory or full visual attention to directions. However, by this time they start to be able to spontaneously transfer their listening skills. They begin moving progressively to the stage where they only need to look at the speaker if they find that instructions are difficult to understand.

Two-channelled attention occurs around the time of Reception entrance. Children can absorb verbal directions related to what they are doing without stopping to look at the speaker. In this respect they are ready to cope with the type of teaching that occurs in class. About a year later integrated attention is well established and well maintained and children can cope with all types of school learning.

Consequences of poor listening skills

Therefore, within early learning settings there will be children who lack flexibility within their attention control. Although many children pass through these developmental stages of attention with ease and cope with the required daily listening demands, there will be others who need to learn about listening by practising it in simple activities. Adults, both in the home and in the learning setting, can help children to remember to listen and to learn to listen. If children have poor listening skills then the following can occur:

- poor development of understanding;
- poor development of spoken language;
- poor development of speech sounds;
- problems with following instructions, especially within a group situation.

Poorly developed listening skills can affect later auditory and phonological literacy acquisition and thus learning may take place mainly through visual means, i.e. through the eyes rather than through the ears. It is also possible that children with poor listening skills may be thought of as 'naughty' because they are inattentive and fidgety.

Development of understanding

The development of understanding meaning is acquired initially through children listening to the speech of others. It is not possible to enumerate the number of words known or understood by young children through listening to their spoken language. Most children understand more words than they use. The bank of words children understand is termed 'receptive language'. It contains all vocabulary from single common nouns, verbs, prepositions, conjunctions, adjectives and adverbs through to abstract concepts. Babies listen to the timbre of adults' voices and learn to recognise those they know. As they grow older they learn to differentiate between happy and cross tones of voice and they acquire an understanding that when certain speech sounds occur they are linked with familiar objects, such as their names, drinks, their toys, going out, parents. They learn by generalising where language is concerned (e.g. at an early age labelling all men as 'dadda') and then by discriminating and particularising. If they are not often spoken to and are left devoid of much human communication, understanding occurs very slowly.

The majority of children have more communicative language experiences in the home rather than in the early years or school settings because of the individual attention they can receive at home. However, even within the home, adults spend a great deal of time directing children rather than interacting with them in any sustained dialogue. It is only when children use language expressively within speech that they have previously received, internalised and understood that adults can discern how much receptive understanding of language children have acquired.

Consequences of receptive language difficulties

If children have problems acquiring sufficient and competent receptive language, the following consequences can occur for later learning:

- adequate expressive language does not develop;
- an inability to follow instructions occurs because of poor understanding;
- an inability to follow stories and discussion and to take in information is noted;

- an ability to contribute appropriately to discussion does not occur;
- building on present vocabulary to acquire new vocabulary does not take place;
- reading may become mechanical because there will be difficulties with contextual clueing and guesswork;
- there may be the development of avoidance strategies as the children become fidgety and distracted or, conversely, even over-helpful;
- boredom and confusion may result;
- signs of poor self-esteem are seen.

Competence in acquiring receptive language

After children have acquired competent receptive language, they have to develop meaningful links between words – to make analogies between words. In order to do this they have to develop a full understanding of all words used, then to apply this knowledge of words from one situation to another and, in order to show they understand, they have to access the appropriate words for speech. Many children with language difficulties or who are slow to develop language appear to have problems establishing these connections. Their understanding is weak, they have word-finding difficulties and their thought processes are inflexible. Semantic properties of language (understanding of meaning) require children to attain understanding of the following:

- function or purpose of the word or the concept (asking the questions 'what is it for?', 'what does it do?', 'how does one use it?');
- location ('where does one find this?');
- attributes or characteristics of the word or the concept (which is 'what might it be made of?', 'what features does it have?');
- category or classification ('what group is it in?').

It is most important that children are given as many opportunities as possible to practise their expressive language. If this occurs, they rehearse the receptive language they have internalised.

Chapter 3
The development of oral language

Expressive language is dependent upon receptive language and develops alongside it. It involves the production of speech sounds as well as coping with content and meaning. It can be stated that expressive language, using speech to communicate, is central, not only to reading and writing, but to all aspects of children's learning. This reiterates the importance of all language functions working together.

Speech sounds
Babies start with 'babbling'. From around nine months onwards their sounds begin to become more consistent and uniform. These sounds can correspond to and be interpreted as the production of first words. These first words can express many meanings, with very young children using one label for similar objects or people (e.g. all animals may become 'dog'). In early speech children may simplify the pronunciation of words, especially if these contain many sounds and they reduce the sounds in clusters of consonants into words that begin with a single consonant (e.g. 'poon' for 'spoon').

The production of speech sounds is also a developmental process and the following generation of these sounds can be observed as children progress through the early years settings:

* all common vowel sounds and the consonants 'p/b/t/d/m/n/w' – acquired by the majority of children by three years;

* the consonants 'k/g/f/h/y' – acquired by the majority of children by four years;

* consonant blends/clusters 'bl/cl/fl/gl/pl/qu/br/cr/dr/fr/gr/pr/tr' at the beginnings of words and consonant blends/clusters at the ends of words 'ks/ls/ms/ps/ts/vs' – acquired by most children by four to four and a half years;

- consonant 's' and 'ng' (as in 'sing') and consonant blends/clusters at the beginning and ends of words 'sp/sm/sn/sk/sl/sw/st' – acquired by the majority of children by five years;

- consonant clusters 'str/skr/spl/spr/thr/shr' – acquired around five years;

- consonant 'l' and consonant clusters 'sh/ch/j/z/v' – acquired by the majority of children by six years;

- 'r/th/th' and 'z' (as in 'measure') – acquired by the majority of children by seven years.

Although children develop at different rates, parents (and within this book the word 'parent' embodies all carers) and early years educators should be aware of these stages so that children's developmental progress is noted. Being able to pronounce certain combinations of speech sounds is important for later phonological work and reading. Mispronunciation can have implications for later work on spelling, especially if children just use sound-symbol matching.

Language acquisition

Problems with sound production need not prevent children wanting to speak and express their meaning. They know what they want to say even though the listener may find it difficult to interpret this. There are stages within the process of language acquisition. These are:

Reception

This stage has already been discussed and described, as it is concerned with increasing children's verbal information and their understanding of language. Efficient receptive processes require competent abilities of attention (listening), selection (choosing the correct sound or word) and discrimination (coping with the difference between sounds and words).

Processing

This is the bridge between received language and expressive language. It refers to the organisation and classification of incoming information and it involves auditory memory processes, the formation of concepts and increasing the store of language within the individual's thought processes. This internal language of thought then links with speech.

Expression

This is concerned with all forms of verbal communication. It involves knowledge and use of vocabulary, syntax (grammar) and meaning. It uses language that is descriptive, judgemental and comparative.

Sage sets out this model of language development slightly differently in *Class talk: successful learning through effective communication* (Sage, 2000). She presents a range of ages to the stages that start at birth and continue well into the school setting. From birth to 15 months (sensory/motor stage) language development includes receptive awareness where young children learn to discriminate rhythm and tone, and the co-ordination of motor skill movements of breathing and sound-making which prepare for the production of first words. Children at this stage begin to link the word with objects and events. It should be noted that any hearing problem at this stage puts children into an 'at risk area' where the basic foundations of language are concerned as they may hear incorrectly and thus speak incorrectly.

The next stage (functional use of words) goes up to four years of age where categorisation and naming of objects, people and events takes place rapidly. Children ask questions which begin with 'what/when/where/who' and start to understand more demanding concepts. It is important at this stage for adults to model language effectively. From four to seven years (the stage of outer speech) children verbalise their thought processes. They think out loud. Because of this need for articulation Sage suggests that silent reading is not effective as children need to read out loud in order to hear what they are saying. Their questioning shows advancement and they begin to explore ideas and use question words starting with 'how' and 'why'. Her final stage from seven years onwards (the stage of inner speech and reading) indicates that by this time internalisation takes place and thought processes become more abstract.

In whichever way the acquisition of language is presented, it can be seen that it is a complicated process. Children have to acquire many skills in order to use language effectively. Within the receptive and processing areas they think and plan messages. Expressively they use speech sounds to produce words and sentences and these are delivered with appropriate tone, volume, expression and even additional gestures. When receiving messages children look at gestures and facial expressions and they listen to the volume, tone and expression given to the words and the sentences. They have to understand the message and process it and may then ask questions to find out more information. Messages can also be stories where children select their own ideas and words and use imaginative thought with as much detail as possible. They then tell these stories to an audience. Conversely children listen to others telling stories. They interpret the messages. They understand. The whole area of expressive language is bound up with what is received and known.

Thus children use language to direct and organise themselves. They use it to shape their thinking. Within developmental receptive and expressive language acquisition the following learning processes are important:

Explaining and making known personal needs

This is sometimes labelled 'self-maintaining' or 'instrumental'. It is the expression of children's material needs where sounds and gestures will also be used. It is the egocentric language of demand. Young children say 'dink' (for 'drink') when they are thirsty and as they grow older the phrase 'I want' is often used.

Directing own actions and actions of others

This is also termed 'regulatory'. Children discover that they can control the behaviour of others through the use of language in the same way as others try to control them. They hear 'do as I tell you' from adults and they use the same tactics themselves. Within this also comes the 'interactional' aspect of language. Here children learn through communication to relate socially with others, usually their family and close friends. Within this learning process the listener might hear family language and jargon which may not be readily understood by others outside the family circle. It is personal to a close-knit group.

Reporting and describing events in experience, categorising events by relating what is new to what has been known previously and coping with outlining events in sequence

Children learn to extract important concepts and to connect one idea to another. Within this process comes the learning function which is used to explore and find out. Children use a wide variety of questioning and from the given answers they learn to categorise, discover and analyse. This is the curiosity that leads to discovery learning. It is the 'tell me why' aspect of language experience.

Personal language or internalisation of ideas working towards logical reasoning

Here children express their feelings about things in the environment. They react to these and show interest. By expressing their own opinions and judgements they reflect the way their identity is evolving.

Prediction leading to recognising cause and effect

Children learn to anticipate events and to recognise that there are alternative courses of action. They make judgements by weighing the evidence they are given.

Projecting or understanding the feelings of others

Children learn why others act as they do and they also learn to put themselves into situations that they have never personally experienced.

Imagining leading from projecting

Children develop imaginary play through words and actions. Children's pretend play, made-up stories, the world of make-believe and the world of fantasy arrives from their exploration of events that are outside what is really happening. They build on prediction and creativity. Children are enabled through role-play to learn about the real-life situations upon which make-believe is based. Children can only develop their ideas through something they have experienced, whether this is from books, poetry or adult's stories. 'Let's pretend' is an important part of language experience.

Informative language enabling children to pass on information
The passing on of information dominates adult's use of language. Adults, especially educators, impart information that they expect children to assimilate. Being able to receive and transmit information is an important skill for children to develop through the other language processes in order to be expressively competent.

The above is a compilation of propositions which are discussed in more detail by writers such as Halliday and Tough (see references).

Possible reasons for language difficulties
It has often been discussed whether or not there has been a general decline in children's language skills. There seem to be those children who find it very hard to express themselves using many of the language processes listed above and especially to play imaginative games. It has been theorised that one reason could be television and there has been some research to back this (Ward, 1992). Television has a positive side, for if children's viewing is well selected it can bring beneficial and helpful information both in exciting and stimulating concrete/visual terms and well-presented auditory terms. However, without parental control television can be negative. Children can become passive, gaining from neither visual nor auditory stimuli, and viewing can take up their time when more active or positive activities could be taking place. When watching television children cursorily watch the visual images and filter out many of the spoken words. Without adults to back up information and explain vocabulary and ideas children can receive a distorted version of what is seen. Unfortunately, there are often more videos in homes than books. Children should not be left to watch television on their own too often. Adults need to watch and discuss with them. There are good programmes that are:

- designed to stimulate interest in a wide variety of topics, where children gain information and where they add to their language bank;

- designed to entertain and educate, where children learn as above;

18

- designed to have a bias to early reading or mathematics, forming a bridge between home and learning situations;
- designed to tell stories, where children can project and imagine;
- of general interest.

Parents need to look at television programmes through the eyes of children and try to imagine the impression that is being made on children's more limited understanding. Parents should see the parts that need explanation so that these will make sense. Television, therefore, should, where possible, be a shared experience. It is the shared experience and the shared discussion that makes television a good medium for learning.

As with television, the radio is also invaluable. This also needs to be a shared experience but the messages received need to become visual experiences in children's imaginations. Some children find this type of visualisation most difficult to experience.

Healy in *Endangered Minds: Why Children Don't Think and What We Can Do About It* (Healy, 1990) postulates that 'children are not speaking properly because they're not hearing words pronounced slowly.' Conversation and explanations on television, as well as those of many adults, are presented rapidly without children being given the time to internalise meaning or process the words accurately.

The development of grammar

In order to use expressive language effectively not only do children have to acquire knowledge of vocabulary, but also have to acquire grammatical knowledge and usage. Studies in the development of children's language show that the acquisition of grammar is also a developmental and sequential process. Webster and McConnell (1987) give detailed and informative explanations about the way children master this aspect of language in their book *Children with Speech and Language Difficulties*. As with any developmental sequence it has to be remembered that children differ and any age levels are arbitrary. Adults in the early years settings need to observe and listen to the children in their charge and they also can gain information from parents about pre-setting language development.

The first stage, which occurs from about nine to 18 months, indicates that very young children begin with sentences with one word components. Children need to talk about objects around them which have some importance to them and their vocabulary builds up to about 50 words by about 24 months. Gesture is used and some intonation is heard. Single words might indicate different wishes depending upon how they are spoken (e.g. 'dink' for 'drink' meaning 'I want a drink', 'take my drink away', 'I see a drink' etc.) In the second stage, which lasts up to around 24 months, these single words start to be linked to make the beginning of sentences. Children join two words such as 'baby sleep', 'mummy read', 'daddy gone'. As with single words some phrases such as 'daddy car' can have more than one meaning (e.g. 'Daddy's gone to work in his car', 'this is Daddy's car' or even 'I want to go in Daddy's car'). Some negative forms will have been learnt such as putting 'no' or 'not' in front of a word (e.g. 'no drink'). This is the time when some question words such as 'where' and 'what' might be used (e.g. 'where doggy?'). Children also continue to use non-verbal gestures to convey meaning.

Up to 30 months in the third stage sentences begin to be built up so that three component words are used. Children learn to use function words such as prepositions and pronouns that enable them to link words and state more detailed information. Word endings such as plural forms and past tenses are used. At this stage children start to hypothesise from what they hear. In this way they experiment with words. Therefore, there may be mistakes as they use the incorrect word. Also there may be errors when using irregular verbs because they generalise from what they have previously learned ('breaked/runned' etc.). It is also easier for children to use the past tense than the future tense. Although adverbs may be used they also may be applied incorrectly. There is continued use of negatives, and questions become more complex and varied.

By the end of the fourth and fifth stages, at around three years of age, children's sentences become longer and increase to four or more structured components. By this age most children have acquired and can use simple sentences and commands. Also they have mastered many of the rules for changing words. Basic grammatical patterns are established but there are still inconsistencies. They begin to use complex sentences and can link separate clauses with 'and'. Later on other connectives are used.

Around the time children enter early years settings from three and a half to four years they may have progressed to using sentences that can be extended and interrelated. If this is so, they are well on the way to coping successfully with oral expression. Most children by this time have understood how varied language can be and they can use it quite effectively although they still have much to learn and experience if they are to master the adult system efficiently. Irregular verbs, the structure of nouns and agreement among words have to be practised and acquired. There is a considerable body of knowledge to learn where the complexities of spoken language are concerned. Even at seven years some children have considerable difficulty understanding and using sentences in the passive form. Words that seem to have no fixed meaning such as 'it/that/who' can be misinterpreted. However, children continue to experiment with and consider language for its own sake. They find pleasure in using words and discovering what language can do.

It has been found that grammatical development and the length of phrases or sentences spoken can be a good measure of children's later literacy performance. If language problems can be resolved in early years settings before more formalised schooling occurs then normal development of later literacy takes place. However, if these language problems persist beyond the age of five and a half years then in all probability these children will have difficulties with reading and written work as they grow older. It has also been noted that there is a close relationship between verbal comprehension (receptive language) and reading comprehension.

Consequences of expressive language difficulties
    If children have problems acquiring adequate and competent expressive language, there may be issues occurring for ease of later learning. Children may:
    • be unable to contribute to conversations and discussions;

- be unable to show what they know;
- be unable to communicate their messages;
- have difficulties establishing and maintaining friendships;
- be unable to express their fears and anxieties, delights and pleasures;
- withdraw from situations where communication is needed;
- show signs of frustration;
- need to develop alternative ways of communicating their message;
- be poor at written language as this will reflect their spoken language;
- have poor reasoning, prediction, sequencing and inference that will show both when reading and writing.

Links with written language and reading

Spoken language underpins the development of written language so poor expressive skills will hold back the development of written skills. The majority of children start school with satisfactory receptive understanding and adequate expressive social and conversational skills as seen in the first stages of language acquisition, but there are particular oral and receptive skills that are necessary for written language. These are:

- the children's ability to concentrate for extended periods of time on stories and other forms of verbal information;
- the ability to discriminate syllables, rhymes and sounds in words (see below for explanation of phonological awareness);
- competence in extended speaking, being able to describe immediate experience, ability in retelling stories and in anticipating events.

Maturation and experience are of importance and few children will have the above established before the age of four, however good their conversational language is or how well they have been exposed to various types of language, books and other forms of writing. Many of the component skills may need regular practice up to the age of six years and beyond. It is felt that boys may be slower to establish competent linguistic skills than girls, and so might those children who have had limited language experiences, who have not had stories read to them or had little experience of extended talk.

There are countries that do not start formal education until the age of seven years. In these countries, the emphasis is on the the the following:

- children need to learn how to share and co-operate;

- children should be prepared for group learning;

- children have to build up their attentional and memory skills;

- children need to develop listening and speaking skills;

- children have to build the vocabulary that will be needed for the more formal teaching of literacy, language and reading.

Children in school should not be expected to read words and sentences that they cannot articulate nor to write ideas that they cannot as yet express. Competence in reading and writing is fundamental to formal educational progress in all subject areas and if children are expected to read and write before their spoken language is developed then this is more of a hindrance than a help in the acquisition of literacy.

To reiterate, if children have problems in acquiring receptive language they may:

- become mechanical readers with poor understanding;

- lack experience where concepts and vocabulary are concerned;

- have poor use of expressive language to reason and work things out.

If they have problems with expressive language they may:

- have poor skills of prediction when reading;

- have poor sentence formation when speaking and writing;

- show restricted use of vocabulary when speaking and writing;

- write as they speak.

Helping young children to become competent and confident where speaking and listening are concerned should be of particular importance in the work of early years educators. The significance of these two areas of language should not be glossed over as they are fundamental to later learning.

Chapter 4
Learning to read

For most children, reading has to be taught. Although some children seem to acquire reading in an osmotic type of way, for the majority learning to read is a time-consuming process. Young children and beginner readers tend to be visual cluers as they see words as blocks of letters and as shapes or patterns. They do not readily understand that there are sounds in words and that there are letter combinations that correspond to these different spoken sounds. Children have to be taught these skills. Like other language areas reading is developmental and it needs skilful teaching and support. Because children have to make sense of the reading process, educators and parents must make sure that children understand both what is read to them and what they can read themselves once the process is started. Thus adults should help children by making reading easy, especially in the early stages. Self-confidence must start early.

Skills for reading

Learning to read is dependent upon adequate speech processing skills. It links with both receptive and expressive language. Speech processing involves:

- auditory discrimination and understanding of incoming verbal information;

- accessing sound patterns (phonology), meaning (semantics) and writing (orthographic representations) of words which are known to them and which are acquired from others' responses and from what they see reproduced in books;

- producing spoken responses to what is seen and then 'translated' on the page.

The manipulation of language is essential to reading. The search for meaning must be there from early beginnings. Reading to children daily will enhance their language skills. Telling stories to children will do likewise.

Using picture books for increasing language knowledge helps with learning to read. However, there are many reasons why learning to read might prove difficult. There has to be the total interaction between the areas of language (expressive and receptive) and literacy (reading and writing). All aspects of language and literacy enrich each other. The knowledge of one improves the other. Reading and writing depend upon speaking and listening. Thus language and literacy develop together. Shared writing can involve shared reading and can include interactive discussion. Phonic work supports the blending of graphemes for reading and the segmentation of phonemes for spelling. It requires competent listening skills and adequate pronunciation skills. It is impossible to read without using other language areas and skills.

What is reading?

Reading is a collection of skills. It can be described as:

- decoding the printed visual symbol (the black mark, the squiggle on the page) into a spoken word;

- understanding expressive language, language that is written on a page;

- an appreciation of great literature and the cultural heritage it represents. This is a higher order reading skill;

- a continuous process which goes way beyond the early years level;

- cracking a code, the symbolic way of recording speech and then interpreting it;

- a selective process where receptive language, understanding of words etc. is important as is visual clueing;

- a pyscholinguistic guessing game where ideas can be accepted or rejected in order to make sense of the words on the page;

- an enjoyable experience which can be solitary or shared.

The development of reading behaviour

As with listening and speaking, reading also develops through developmental stages. These stages begin with children sharing books with adults and ends with independence in coping with unknown texts. There are different examples of how reading develops and the model below draws on the one offered by Waterland (1985) in her book *Read With Me: An Apprenticeship Approach to Reading*. The stages can overlap depending on the books used and the maturity of the children.

At first stories are read by adults to children and the children look at the pictures when listening to the story. Once they understand that messages and enjoyment occurs from books they will be encouraged to look at the pictures and writing (the text) as they listen. Still listening to the story, children start to join in with the adult which shows an understanding of the meaning and some continuity with recalling the words. In this shared experience children begin to repeat the words, learn the words, make up the story or even 'read' words correctly.

The next stage involves children communicating with stories that they know (early reading) when still working with adults. They may 'make up' the story. There need not be any looking at the print, pointing to the words, reading words that match with the text or even recalling the word order correctly. Once this is seen to be acceptable, children may start to retell the story quite accurately but there is no pointing or word match although they are mindful of the text, the symbols on the page. From this basis then, children start to retell the story quite accurately and they begin to use their fingers to point along the lines until they can accurately tell the story with the beginnings of word and speech matching. At times their reading appears very fluent. Children will read those words they know and guess the others.

The final stage involves children coping with texts that are new to them which is the beginning of actual reading. They start by reading those words they know and guessing the others. At times they appear to be quite fluent and they will use word-finger matching. At other times they are hesitant. Their knowledge of recognised words will grow. Because of increased fluency and because they have acquired skills taught to them by adults, they will try to use contextual cueing, phonic decoding and visual generalisation to work out unknown words. These methods can often be inaccurate at first and children's reading seems to become less fluent and they may slow down to reading word by word with no expression. However, as reading develops and systematic teaching takes place, children will acquire more known words, they will decode unknown ones with accuracy and they will become proficient in using reliable strategies. There are fewer unknown words and these are tackled with confidence. Reading becomes more fluent and expression is used.

It must be noted that where the children seem to be on the above set of stages depends on the books they are given to work with. Although the acquisition of reading can be said to be developmental, there are no age levels given and children show different reading behaviours even during the course of reading one book.

Problems for the acquisition of reading

Because of the complexities of learning to read, there are language acquisition barriers or problems which might get in the way and which will need help and support. These are:

• poor concentration; • difficulty with listening and attention, particularly in groups; • problems understanding vocabulary; • low levels of language acquisition.	If these are present they may lead children to not being able to attain meaningful understanding of book language and the structure of stories.
• very basic vocabulary; • basic sentence construction; • speech difficult or impossible to understand.	These will lead to problems being understood when reading or problems when attempting contextual guesswork.
• poor auditory skills; • problems linking letter sound and letter shape; • over-use of the visual approach to acquiring words for reading.	If children are found to have these difficulties they may have later problems with learning phonic decoding and with the pronunciation of some words.

Reading and the *National Literacy Strategy*

Reading is described in this DfEE (1998) document as a range of strategies used for gaining meaning from a text. It is shown as four searchlights that interact with each other. These are 'knowledge of context', 'phonics', 'grammatical knowledge' and 'word recognition and graphic knowledge'. Within Key Stage 1 it is suggested that 'there should be a strong and systematic emphasis on the teaching of phonics and other word level skills'.

Children have to learn to discriminate between the separate sounds in words, to learn the most common letters and letter combinations and to decode words by using sounds for blending. It is recognised that the 'Reception year is a critical time for building on children's developing literacy' and it is advised that children in this year group are taught systematically even though the Literacy Hour need not be as formal as in later years within the school. Within this formal teaching there should be word level work.

Phonological awareness

Coping with reading is dependent also on good phonological awareness for if this is well developed children find it easier to cope with symbol-sound decoding for reading and sound-symbol encoding for spelling. Phonological awareness is concerned with the system of speech sounds and the range of speech sounds that make up the language system. It refers particularly to children's understanding that the linked speech sounds that make up spoken language can be broken down into smaller segments and that these segments can be manipulated. Word-sound play can then occur. When children cope with this system of speech sounds, they can recognise that words have boundaries within sentences and that syllables have boundaries within words. They learn that individual phonemes (sounds) make up words and part words and they recognise how they can be aware of these.

Phonological awareness evolves through the children's development of speech and language from the early stages. Phonological awareness training should begin within the foundation level and should be continued until children can decode and encode accurately. It is necessary to develop phonological awareness in *all* children rather than leaving its development to chance. Without its development the manipulation of phonics may not take place.

Decoding and encoding use phonics, which is a system for linking individual speech sounds, termed 'phonemes', with written letters or letter patterns called 'graphemes'. When phonic instruction is developed as part of the whole programme of reading and writing, more competent achievement in word recognition, spelling and vocabulary is reached.

The goals of phonic instruction are to help children develop an understanding of the spelling sound correspondence in the English writing system and to help children learn to recognise frequent words and spelling patterns automatically at a glance. There are two methods of working with phonic teaching. One is systematic teaching of individual sounds in order to build up, make and read words. The other is using existing known words and examining these and breaking them down into their component sounds. Whichever is used, working on phonological awareness leads to competence in phonics.

Components of phonological awareness

• alliteration	understanding that words can have the same beginning sound pattern (phoneme) and being able to generate such words
• rhyming	understanding the concept that there can be 'sound' patterns in words and being able to match rhyming pictures, say nursery rhymes, complete a rhyming couplet, generate rhyming words and other rhymes
• segmentation	understanding that words contain syllables or beats and being able to segment 2-syllable words into their syllables, segmenting polysyllabic words into their correct number of syllables, splitting syllables into onset and rime and coping with phonemic awareness (segmenting syllables into their component phonemes)
• blending	understanding that words can be split into component sounds and discrete sounds can be synthesised into whole words and being able to join words into compound words, blending syllables into polysyllabic words, joining onset with rime to make words and blending individual phonemes into words
• deletion	understanding that words can be split into smaller parts and being able to omit a word from a compound word, omitting a syllable from a polysyllabic word, omitting the beginning sound in a word, omitting the end sound in a word and omitting a sound within the word

Bryant and Bradley (1985) in *Children's Reading Problems* and Bryant and Goswami (1990) in *Phonological Skills and Learning to Read* state that two of the fundamental phonological skills needed to be well understood and established by children are the ability to recognise rhyme and alliteration. Many studies have been carried out to determine the links between phonological skills and later reading strengths and weaknesses. Layton and Deeny (1996) suggest that there are those children whose poor phonological skills are evidently imbedded within early spoken language difficulties but that there are others whose speech and language difficulties remain hidden.

> 'Their phonological weaknesses may not be identified in the pre-school years because there are very few specific tasks or games which provide opportunities for demonstrating explicit phonological awareness at this early age.' (page 131)

It is, therefore, most important that children are given these opportunities and that assessment of phonological awareness is set firmly in place within the early years settings.

Phonological skills at the before reading stage
It is recognised that average children in the early years setting can:

- match spoken words by alliteration;

- match spoken words by rhyme;

- provide a rhyme at the end of a spoken, predictable sentence;

- orally blend phonemes into words (although this skill is not consistent);

- clap beats in some multi-syllabic words (usually words that have a strong beat and that are well-known to the children);

- represent initial and/or final consonants in invented spelling.

Phonological skills at the early reading stage
Building on the above, Reception and Year 1 children can:

- generate rhymes from a given word;

- segment simple onsets and rimes;

- begin to make orthographic analogies in reading (being aware of letter strings which have a 'sound' component);

- increase their ability to represent consonants in writing and begin to use vowels within spellings (although not necessarily the correct ones).

Reading connected to expressive language

It has to be remembered that children's speech sounds develop over time (see the section in expressive language about the production of speech sounds). There will be some actual sounds, phonemes, that young children may be unable to pronounce so this has to be kept in mind when oral work on sounds is taking place.

Also children's ability to guess at unknown words is dependent upon their syntactic and semantic abilities. If they can use words that describe others (adjectives and adverbs) and correctly understand function words such as conjunctions and prepositions, and if they can comprehend how words work grammatically together, then they will be better placed to read for meaning or to guess words. Also the wider their total vocabulary is, the more efficient their contextual clueing will be. As children become more proficient at decoding, it is sometimes seen that they can 'read' more than they understand because of words not being within their store of knowledge.

Similarities between reading and listening

Reading and listening:

- are both 'input' activities. When reading, children take in information through their eyes, and in listening this comes in through their ears;

- involve thinking, sometimes just with information processing and at others with imaginative thought;

- entail applying what is already known to what is unknown;

- involve the understanding and interpreting of words and groups of words into meaningful experiences;

- require auditory discrimination;

- need some level of concentration and attention;

- can take place for information purposes, for enjoyment or in order to be influenced or persuaded;
- require children to possess the ability to anticipate, guess and hypothesise;
- require some kind of appraisal from time to time. Children should be encouraged to think about the messages rather than just listening to the word sounds;
- involve the children in decisions and questions about who is speaking or writing and why their statements are being made. This is because speakers and writers require readers and listeners to perform at varying levels.

Chapter 5
The development of writing skills

Writing is a skill of communication. It carries messages – either personal or shared by many others. Messages can be simple and functional like writing memos, lists or cards or more extensive as with letters or even far more extended pieces of written work which produce informative pieces of writing. Speaking and writing are output activities. Writing reflects spoken language as it relies on the performer's ability to place words and sentences together correctly and appropriately. Writing to standard English requirements mirrors an oral knowledge and an expressive competence of standard English. The *National Curriculum for English* (DfE, 1995) states 'Differences between spoken and written forms relate to the spontaneity of speech and to its function in conversation, whereas writing is more permanent, often carefully crafted, and less dependent upon immediate responses.'

The *National Literacy Strategy* philosophy is for writing to be taught explicitly, with teachers being expected to model, guide, observe and coach learners towards maturity. Writing contains three skills. One is the physical skill of *handwriting* which may change to word processing at a later date. The second is learning correctness in *spelling*, while the third is coping with *content*, the expressive side. But writing is hierarchical in its structure and can only be developed from what children already know. Cursive writing can only be achieved if children can form letters in print correctly. Paragraphs come after sentences, sentences are formed from words in spoken language, words are used according to word knowledge, and spelling is learnt in a staged approach.

Because of the additional physical skills required for handwriting, it is usually felt that writing is the most difficult element of the four language components to master.

Elements within writing

In the English language, writing:

• embodies marks which are arranged horizontally on paper;

• is arranged from left to right across the page;

• is set out in horizontal lines which follow each other down the page from top to bottom;

• is made up of particular symbols;

• contains symbols which are finite in number;

• has symbols which are used again and again;

• is formed in a particular way so that each symbol has a slightly different shape and configuration;

• has symbols which have names allocated to them;

• is composed of groups of symbols which form words;

• can form words that can be memorised and retained in the memory and later reproduced as required.

Writing, like the other strands of language, is acquired from learning by doing. It is best learned if children are encouraged to compose their own words and texts from very early ages. Before children are able to produce any written work that is recognisable, they are taking in information about the writing system. Here is a link between reading and writing. From books and other read material children can form impressions about what writing looks like and what writing represents.

Very young children explore writing implements on any surface. This is neither drawing nor writing and has been termed 'undifferentiated scribble'. Young children, even those of Reception age, find it hard to describe the difference between drawing and writing as they do not really know the difference between these words. However, they have internalised that there is a difference between these two activities and can usually point to 'drawing' or 'writing' if shown examples of these presentations but they might use both within an activity. As children become more exposed to written material through books, they start to display more 'conventional' type marks within their written or drawing work. Once individual letters are used, children quite quickly produce whole words. They start to 'read' their attempts and make stories or sentences about these even if to the adult the words are not recognisable. This mirrors the way children make up texts when reading.

Children learn to recognise that:

• written text carries meaning which other people can read;

• the writer is the one who decides what the meaning is;

• the writer must learn to use certain conventions if readers are to understand their meaning.

The components of writing within the *National Literacy Strategy*
Writing is included within the three strands:

• word level	Within this strand are found the acquisition of motor skills for correct letter formation, the spatial awareness of placing letters correctly in relation to lines on the page, the spelling of words which involves employing both visual memory and phonemic encoding, and using spacing between words to form separate entities.
• sentence level	This comprises children's knowledge of how spoken words make up logical sentences, the understanding and use of punctuation, and children's understanding of when to use upper and lower case letters.
• text level	Here occurs the grouping of sentences in paragraphs, the sequencing of paragraphs into longer text, the knowledge of the audience in order to write the piece to its correct purpose and function, and being able to reflect on how the sentences and words form part of the whole text.

Because of the close relationship between writing and reading, the National Literacy framework makes sure that the range of activities undertaken for writing are similar to those for reading. It points out that the phonic element taught within word level for reading will be equally necessary for the skills of spelling. There is emphasis in the Reception year on shared writing activities and early composition.

Children learn conventions such as:
- the layout of their 'scribble' differentiates it from their drawing;
- 'scribble' and then writing goes from left to right across the page;
- 'scribble' and then writing goes in parallel lines across the page and covers the whole page;
- there is differentiation between the use of upper or lower case letters;
- numbers are rarely written alongside letters.

Stages in acquiring writing skills

At first children represent their messages by drawing and they will tell the story or the message. Adults might write for them in order to model or show what the message would look like in print.

Writing in the early stages

Gorman and Brooks (1996) have identified seven stages of early writing development. The first five usually occur before the work of the *National Literacy Strategy* starts. These are:

• Stage One	This is the stage of drawing and sign writing, scribbles and shapes which contain little resemblance to letters but children know the difference between what they draw in pictures and what they 'write' in words.
• Stages Two, Three and Four	Within these stages the children learn to form the shapes of individual letters, their writing starts to resemble English symbols and there may be spaces placed between groups of letters. The children write over and then copy the adult's writing. This copying of writing gradually results in them writing letters correctly without help. Then they are ready to compose.

Another way of describing this set of features in the way children develop text composition is as follows, adapted from *Beginning Writing* by John Nicholls et al (1989):

• cursive 'graffiti' (the scribble stage)	This has no meaning for the reader although the reader might be expected to supply meaning. With encouragement the children realise that they have to 'read' their messages in order to communicate with the reader.
• printed 'graffiti'	Again there is no meaning for the reader and the children have to supply this. However, there is a difference between the formation of the pencil marks on the page with less loose random scribbling.
• letter sequences combined with 'graffiti'	Again the reader cannot interpret the messages so the children have to supply these. However, there are some recognisable letter shapes on the page. Often these are the first capital letter of the child's own name.
• words combined with 'graffiti' and other letters and letter sequences	An occasional word can be read amid the other symbols. These may be the children's own names and the first learnt words. Still the children have to read their messages to the reader.
• short phrases or sentences	Children begin to label their drawings or write their own messages. Some words are spelt correctly while others show some symbol-sound correspondence in a very early stage of phonemic development and some words may be represented by their initial letters. The reader is able to make some sense of the writing.

Chapter 6
Developing communication skills
in early years settings

The importance of play

Early years settings help children to acquire skills through organised activities and play. Although the settings may seem noisy and often randomly arranged to the uninitiated, the organisation of the set activities has been carefully prepared and the play is purposeful. The DES document *Starting with Quality* (1990) states:

'For young children purposeful play is an essential and rich part of the learning process. Play is a powerful motivator, encouraging children to be creative and to develop their ideas, understanding and language. Through play children explore, apply and test out what they know and can do.' (page 7)

Through play children can acquire and improve the following skill areas related to language:

- using all their senses (hearing, seeing, doing) especially those required for early reading and writing activities;
- understanding (internalisation of) new vocabulary and concepts;
- acquiring, increasing and practising word usage (new vocabulary and concepts);
- extending sentence construction;
- building up thoughts and ideas through creative and imaginative experiences;
- improving questioning;
- gaining independence;
- helping with concentration;
- learning to be social and co-operative.

Learning through play is a non-threatening situation. Although it can challenge and extend children's learning experiences and can consolidate prior learning, it is both enjoyable and motivating. Within play children cannot easily compare their efforts with those of their peers so they more readily take risks and experiment with learning.

It is important that as much oral language is encouraged as possible. In the formal environment of a school classroom, however, children are given fewer opportunities to talk – in fact, talk is often actively discouraged. This is less so in early years settings.

Children usually speak more at home if they have the full attention of one adult, but often there are times when they are engaged in solitary silent activities. However, in early years settings children should be able to enjoy many opportunities for interactive talk. They will have others with whom they can speak in play activities and in social situations. There are also adults who can help take children's communication forward, adults who will model language and extend understanding and expression.

As well as setting up structured play activities to facilitate learning, adults in the early years settings need to organise learning situations that will set suitable learning challenges for all children. In order to do this the settings should enhance and encourage children to undertake new activities and, therefore, increase their knowledge, skills and understanding. Although play is most desirable, children also need to learn to concentrate, so some activities can be set as individual 'challenges' where the learner has to work on a task for a given length of time. Group or class-based activities can also help children to concentrate.

Children need to be motivated, not just with activities they particularly enjoy but within all learning situations. Therefore, the adults have to be aware through observational techniques how long particular children can work on an activity and how more challenging tasks can be made interesting and motivating. Also through observational and assessment techniques adults need to be aware of children's strengths and weaknesses and to be able to set targets for increasing their learning.

Where learning takes place

Although early years settings will differ depending on size, location, number of children, number of staff and age-range of the children, there are certain areas of activity within the settings that can be used to enhance learning which are common to all. Because listening, speaking, reading and writing are connected to each other and work with each other, in order that children become fully literate at some time in their educational careers, all learning activities, wherever they take place, will utilise one or more of these four skills. Listening does not only occur when children are seated at their tables with the adult speaking or reading a story to them and reading does not occur only at story time or in the book corner. Adults will use their judgements as to which literacy skill could be enhanced when children are working in the:

- book area;

- sand area;

- water area;

- painting area;

- home corner;

or using:

- puppets;

- malleable materials;

- construction toys;

- paper and pen/pencil/coloured crayons/felt-tip pens/wax crayons;

or working at:

- music;

- PE;

- outdoor play;

- role play;

- more 'formal' style lessons;

or:

• having their playtime snack;

• eating lunch.

The suggestions in the second section of this book for enhancing the skills of listening, speaking, reading and writing can occur when any of the above activities are taking place.

The role of the adult

In order to promote children's learning, adults in the early years settings act as:

Providers

As providers they set up rich and informative classrooms that promote active learning, where there are opportunities for all the above activities to take place, where children can work and play co-operatively or independently, where there is the chance for them to be alone as well as being with peers. Teachers in these settings will work with other adults, nursery nurses, support assistants, volunteers and parents, and these other adults will work co-operatively with each other, undertaking whatever roles are necessary.

Models

As models adults will extend the children's learning. They will use judicial questioning, help enlarge the children's vocabulary, help lengthen their expressive attempts and co-read either with groups or individuals. They will repeat and reorganise the children's expressive attempts and they will act as 'co-learners' by undertaking some activities alongside the children so that the children hear and see different approaches.

Guides

As guides they will help children choose activities. They will be aware of children's progress in all areas of learning and will carefully direct them in order to advance their learning experiences.

Organisers

As organisers adults will co-ordinate all these experiences within the chosen activities.

Observers/Assessors

As observers/assessors they will become aware of children's strengths and weaknesses, of their likes and dislikes, of their behaviours and personalities and they will choose activities to help any problem area noted.

Although this description of adults working within the early years may seem rather overwhelming, it is what is happening in these settings. Often teachers and other staff give little thought to the multiplicity of their roles. However, it could be a helpful exercise if at staff meetings one aspect is discussed per session and all approaches pertaining to that particular part of the role are thoroughly consulted. If the language areas are added to these then the adults would be able to quantify where learning is being achieved satisfactorily or maybe where it needs some additional input.

Curriculum guidance for the foundation stage

Curriculum guidance for the foundation stage (QCA, 2000) gives general advice on what is involved if effective learning is to take place and what is required for effective teaching in order to promote this learning.

It offers several statements about how children can learn effectively. To summarise, it is suggested that children need to feel safe and confident and should use all their senses in order for learning to take place. Within play and learning activities, they should be encouraged to be creative and imaginative, they need to originate experiences for themselves and they need to be given time to explore their own ideas and interests in as much depth as is possible. It is recognised that children learn in different ways and at differing paces and this should be built into the learning situations. The effectiveness of peer support is also recognised. When children encounter and assimilate learning experiences, they need to learn to make links from these to other learning experiences. It is also implied that activities that enhance effective language development will be beneficial for children's proficiency of learning.

A similar set of statements is set out for teachers. They are expected to be efficient within their teaching by using observational techniques and assessment techniques to inform and plan activities for learning. Teachers need to plan the way the environment of the setting is used so that the children gain maximum benefit from it and evaluate the way it is used. Within the teaching environments all planned activities and experiences need to be challenging but attainable by the learners. Correct behavioural situations should be modelled and children should be helped to gain positive attitudes to learning by adult-children interaction and support being well-planned. Because effective learning can occur through learning from peers, teachers are expected to encourage the children to learn from each other and also to teach each other. Some direct teaching of certain skills and knowledge-bound areas is expected. Language and communication can be supported by teachers using a range of language that extends that of the children, by using correct grammatical constructions and by the judicial use of questioning. Effective teaching is helped by teachers working in partnership with the home.

This document also gives some more specific advice about learning and teaching for the particular areas within the early learning goals. Within the section titled 'communication, language and literacy' effective learning is covered through providing children with:

- time to speak and, therefore, portray their ideas within given activities;

- time to listen;

- opportunities for using all language experiences in every part of the curricular activities;

- a learning environment that provides as many opportunities for communication as is feasible;

- a learning environment that abounds in print.

In order for this to be effective, teachers should:

- understand the importance of talk and alternative forms of communication;

45

- observe children and by doing so plan for situations where they can best develop their speaking and listening;
- help children to develop communicative language through interaction with others;
- observe children in order to help them to understand the processes within reading and writing activities;
- model language and show how it can be used for thinking;
- demonstrate how language is used in reading and writing;
- help children to understand books and how they work;
- be flexible in their planning and knowledgeable about the learning processes;
- work together as a team.

National Curriculum for English

The stepping stones within the early years document give examples of progression for children within the skills areas. However, because the early years settings also includes the Reception year of more 'formal' education, adults working in settings out of school need to be aware of the demands of the *National Curriculum for English.*

Key Stage 1 speaking and listening which is attainment target 1, and which is not separated into two skill areas, builds on the early learning goals. Included here is the use of imaginative language, language used for reporting and using attention for listening and response. In order to gain level 1 for speaking and listening, children should be able to talk about things that pertain to their own interests, to be able to cope with relaying simple messages to different listeners and to speak audibly. Children should start to use some detail as they begin to amplify their ideas or accounts. Children should be able to listen to their peers and adults and respond as appropriate.

The long-term goal for attainment target 2, reading, is that children will learn 'to read with fluency, accuracy, understanding and enjoyment' and in doing so will use a range of strategies. For level 1 children should be able to recognise familiar words and use letter knowledge and sound-symbol relationships in order to read unknown words. They should be able to demonstrate that they use meaning when reading aloud. It is recognised that during these reading activities children will sometimes need adult support. When being read to, children need to be able to articulate why they like or dislike poems, stories and non-fiction texts.

Writing is attainment target 3 and to gain level 1 children start to be able to communicate meaning by writing simple words or phrases. They begin to show that they understand conventions such as the full stop and when they handwrite they can produce letters which are clearly shaped and correctly orientated.

It needs to be reiterated that to become fully literate takes many years and children develop at different rates and have differing strengths and weaknesses. But all children can progress.

Working with parents

During the early years, working in partnership with parents is perhaps more important than at any other time in children's lives. Parents are usually the sole 'educators' of their children until they enter early years settings, playgroup, nursery school or school. What has been mentioned so far in this book and what will be described in future chapters should involve parents and enlist parental support in all learning experiences. It is not helpful to show that some activities can more easily be undertaken by parents and that others should be solely assigned to the early years setting because family circumstances are different and parents have differing strengths, interests and time in order to work and play with their children. The notion of partnership has been written about by educators in many publications.

As the Warnock Report (1978) recognised:

'Parents can be effective partners only if professionals take notice of what they say and how they express their needs, and treat their contributions as intrinsically important.' (para. 9.6)

It has often been stated that partnership cannot be established if educators accept or invite parents to join them on their own 'professional' terms. This implies that the partnership would become one-sided with the parent being felt to have less expertise than the educator: '... a true partnership suggests an acceptance of equal skills and expertise, of an open-minded sharing of knowledge, skills and experience, and a sense that the partner brings something different but of equal value to the relationship' (Pugh, 1985).

Pugh proposes that parents can be expected or invited to work in one of the following six ways:

• non-participation	Here parents are passive either because of lack of confidence, non-understanding or because of a language barrier or because they are deliberately kept away from the 'education' of their children.
• present but not involved	Parents are receptive and responsive to what the educators are doing but they are not actively involved themselves.
• co-operation	This covers involvement of parents usually under the supervision of the teachers/educators. This type of involvement includes in-setting working with children, such as reading stories, and doing some work such as putting up displays, washing up.

• collaboration	Here parents work in a more shared way where they might plan and initiate activities themselves. Overall responsibility still remains with the educators. Working collaboratively can be seen when parents contribute to children's assessment of learning needs and with planning further action.
• partnership	Collaboration and partnership approaches are very similar. However, the latter 'extends to include equal access to information and resources'.
• control	Parents take decisions for action and they have full responsibility for activities and resources.

It might be helpful for staff in early years settings to carry out an informal audit of how they work with parents. Working towards a partnership approach should be the goal. The concept of partnership is enshrined within the sphere of special educational needs where DfEE documents encourage teachers to work closely with parents and this requires a spread to all aspects of education. The early years setting is an ideal place for fostering collaborative and partnership approaches. Parents possess a great deal of knowledge about their own children which should be shared with the adults in the settings. These adults should similarly share their observations and knowledge. The two parties then can work together to help children's learning, with planned and shared ideas.

Chapter 7
Listening activities

As the earlier chapter on listening highlighted, there are developmental stages connected to attention and weaknesses in this area can result in later learning problems because receptive language may be underdeveloped, spoken language may be limited, and reading and spelling through knowledge and use of sounds will be impeded. Therefore, it is most important that there are many listening activities built into the curriculum within the early years settings.

Assessment of listening

Adults should closely observe how children react in the variety of situations and activities that require them to attend and later respond. There may be a difference in the way children react in an individual situation to that of a group or whole class. There may be differences in the way they react when a story is read or when the register is called. They may listen to adults more carefully than when they listen to their peers. Young children may still be in the developmental stage of being single-channelled and they may find it difficult to switch from task to task. Children may seem more alert at a particular time of day and information such as how much sleep they had or whether or not they ate before coming to the early years setting can be helpful.

It is also particularly important to know about children's actual levels of hearing. Many young children have early hearing problems that range from intermittent glue ear when they have colds to more persistent hearing difficulties that might even result in the fitting of grommets. Good liaison with the home is necessary and with the health visitor or nurse.

When activities that require listening skills occur, adults should note what the children are actually doing. Are they fidgeting? Are they looking at the speaker or the stimulus, such as the television or picture? Do they seem to be thinking and internalising what is being said? The latter answer will be based on subjective thought from the adult but sometimes it can be surmised that the children are either not paying attention or understanding as their expressions seem to be non-focused and rather 'blank'. Adults, by a judicial question, can also determine whether attention is fully on the task in hand. Comparing listening behaviours across the class can give some information about a particular individual's competencies. A simple checklist can be devised for the early years setting which can be filled in by any adult over time.

Problems with listening and attention

One reason for not listening may be because the children do not understand the language they are receiving. Questioning them or observing if they comply with particular instructions can be a way of determining whether the adult's spoken language needs to be changed. The following factors can affect the children's abilities to understand spoken information and messages:

Environment

Some children may find a busy and active room too full of interest and noise (even if this is working noise) for them to settle to attending to a task. Even when supposedly focused on listening to a story their attention may be distracted from the book to the colourful and stimulating classroom environment.

Inadequate and briefly given information

Children with auditory processing problems who find it hard to take in and understand information may need repetition and rehearsal of what they have heard and what they have to do.

Information too complex

Children who have immature and undeveloped language systems may find it too difficult to interpret long sentences, complex grammar and unfamiliar vocabulary.

Information presented too quickly

Some children may not be able to hold all the information if the adult talks too fast. They may not be able to differentiate between the word boundaries within sentences and they may not be able to process how individual words are articulated and pronounced.

Not fully aware that listening is important

There may be some children who need to be taught why they should listen. They may have arrived from a home environment where there is little adult-child discussion or story reading and where these children have not been able to see the relevance of sitting quietly and taking in information through their ears. These children will have to learn the consequences of what happens if they listen carefully and what might happen if they do not. The latter should not mean a 'punishment' but how they could miss out on activities etc. if they have not heard what is going to happen. Children can learn from peer role models with adults praising the listeners and making comments about how successful certain children were in listening activities. Praise for the children with listening difficulties is also very important especially if there are comments such as 'you listened very well in story time, well done' or 'I liked the way you paid attention when Mr S... was telling us about his dog' etc. Children with more inattention than attention should practise listening in simple activities at first and adults need to be specific about when listening should occur by beginning activities with some discussion about listening and paying attention so that the children are given gentle reminders.

Activities for listening games

There are many activities that can be built into the everyday curriculum of the early years setting. They can occur as one-off activities or can occur in sessions such as PE or music or can be fitted in to register times or snack times.

Awareness of sound

Listening to silence

Adults tell children to be quiet or silent and children learn that this means that they should not talk. But the concept of silence is difficult because there are so many extraneous noises that get in the way of total quietness.

Children can be asked to keep quiet and still and to listen to any of the little noises that might be coming from elsewhere. These can be discussed afterwards and the adults can see which children have good powers of auditory perception.

What can you hear when...?
Children can be taken for a walk around the school, the playground, outside in the community and when they come back they talk about the sounds they have heard.

What is that noise?
An adult makes a noise (e.g. tap on the desk, rattle the door handle, pull the blinds) and the children have to identify the sound made. These sounds will have to come from behind the children unless one can be sure that they will all keep their eyes closed and not peep!

Which sound is this?
Tapes can be made of sounds within the home or school and these have to be identified when the tape is played. This develops children's abilities to attach meaning and associations to non-verbal noises.

Auditory attention

Can you hear me?
This type of activity is to develop attention control and develop skills of learning to respond to auditory stimuli rather than the visual. Activities would include whispering the children's names and expecting them to respond.

Choose the right sound
The adult makes two sounds for children to listen to (e.g. drum/bell). If these are not on a tape the children have to close their eyes. They are told to signal in a certain way such as putting up their hand when they hear one of the sounds which has been specified at the beginning of the activity.

Listening to a story

As a story is being told the children have to signal when they hear particular words (such as animal names, colours etc.).

Sounds in order

This is a more difficult version of the first activity. The adult makes a noise (such as playing the triangle) which the children have to identify. Then two sounds are made and the children have to identify them and say them in the correct order. This can be attempted with up to about five sounds.

First and last sounds

A tape is made with a collection of noisemakers that make a series of sounds. The children have to recall and say what sound is heard first and what sound is heard last.

Hear/see the mistake

The adult looks at pictures with the children and makes some deliberate errors when describing these. The children have to hear what is wrong and explain. These can be made as simple or as difficult as the adult feels is necessary. (It has the benefit of giving the children some visual clueing as well.)

Hear the mistake

Silly sentences or silly stories are told by the adult (e.g. 'the sun is black in the sky' or 'I use my spoon to clean my teeth'). The children, using only hearing, have to say why the sentence is silly.

Sound location

Where is that noise?

The children (and this can be an individual activity) stand in the middle of the room with their eyes closed. Someone (either the adult or another child) makes a noise (e.g. banging a drum or shaking a tin of buttons) and the individual has to point to where the sound is coming from.

Find that sound

This is a sound treasure hunt. Something that emits continuous noise (such as a clockwork toy, a musical box or a radio) is hidden somewhere in the room. The children have to find its location by listening rather than looking. At first the sounds can be loud but they can be made as quiet as possible so that all the seekers have to be quiet as well.

Sound discrimination

Find its twin

The adult makes pairs of 'shakers' (boxes or tins with similar noises inside such as buttons, sand, peas etc.). When one box is shaken the children have to find its matching pair.

Is it high or low?

Children have to distinguish high and low sounds played on the piano or recorder or made from tapping glasses. Adults can start with very different sounds and then the sounds can be made more similar.

Is it loud or soft?

As with high and low sounds, children listen to a range of noises and determine whether these are loud or soft.

Act on a sound

Children are expected to respond with actions to different tones of voice, for example they tiptoe if the adult whispers or they stamp if the voice is loud.

Follow one sound

This can be a very noisy and complicated activity. A group of children and an adult have to tell an individual to do something. Their instructions are different but they all give this command at the same time. However, the child has to follow the adult's command and no-one else's.

Who is calling my name?

One individual stands in the middle of the group with eyes closed and someone calls out his or her name. The child has to identify the name of the speaker.

Sound sequencing

Sounds in order

The adult makes a noise (such as playing the triangle) which the children have to identify. Then two sounds are made and the children have to identify them and say them in the correct order. This can be attempted with up to about five sounds.

Numbers in order

Playing 'remembering telephone numbers' can help children develop their auditory memories. Start with two numbers and see how many children can remember. Work up to about five or six numbers.

Word sequences

From listening to sounds in order and numbers in order, children can learn to hear, remember and recall words in order. At first they can be given visual clues (e.g. 'I packed my bag' but having a pile of objects which are put in order) and then the game is played using just auditory memory skills. This game can be played with listing names of animals, colours, children's names etc., but it has to be remembered that some children may find the searching for words and their production more difficult than the auditory memory side.

Listening with understanding

What is wrong?

As with auditory attention, the adult tells silly sentences, silly stories, silly ends to sentences, true or false sentences and the children have to explain what is wrong and give the correct word or words. This activity links with expressive language.

What is this riddle?

Children appear to love riddles but often do not understand what they are about. The adult tells some simple riddles and the children discuss their meanings.

Give an answer

Any simple question can be asked and children have to supply the answers. In a group situation this helps with turn taking.

What was the question?

This activity is a variation to the above where simple answers are given and the children have to make up the question that would have been supplied.

Let's finish a sentence

The adult says sentences with the end word missing and the children have to complete them.

Odd word out

Lists of four or five words are given. All but one belong to the same category and the children have to say which is the odd one. They can also be asked why they chose that particular word.

Let's describe the picture

Children make up stories or tell what is in a picture. They should be encouraged to give sentences rather than one word labelling. Here the adult can model sentence structure and amplify answers. This activity also links with expressive language.

How do we describe?

An object is shown and the adult says one word to describe it. The children are asked for other words that mean the same as the given describing word (such as little/tiny/small/titchy).

Let's finish the story

The adult tells a short story and the children listen and complete the story with a suitable ending. Again this links with expressive language.

Let's group the words

Children are helped to understand the group name of particular objects etc. (e.g. 'seagulls, robins, owls and eagles are? ... birds'). This activity can be given the other way round (e.g. 'tell me the names of some birds').

What would you do?
Children are given a circumstance and asked to explain what they would do. This is another activity that links with expressive language.

Listening with understanding activities understandably overlap with expressive language activities because in order to show that children understand meaning they often have to use speech (although there could be some activities where actions show understanding). If it is found that children obviously do not understand heard vocabulary then they may need some direct teaching of words.

Helping with comprehension difficulties
There is a great deal of adult oral language within educational settings whether these are within school or during the early years settings. Adults deliver much information by direct instruction or incidental conversation and other information is gained through the medium of books or the television. Adults should aim for children to take responsibility for understanding these messages. Children need to realise that it is acceptable to have some difficulties and if they feel they cannot always understand then they should ask for explanations.

This chapter has already dealt with the problems that occur when listening and attention skills are limited and ideas for helping the children have been offered. The following give ideas for making it easier for children to comprehend:

- Adults must remember not to speak too quickly as this might overload the children's processing abilities. The rate of speech should be slowed down. However, care should be taken not to make speech too unnatural.

- Long sentences can be divided into shorter and more separate ideas. This helps memory and auditory processing.

- If sentences or words appear to be too complicated then these should be rephrased or simplified. In order to build up vocabulary knowledge it is important to use varied vocabulary and to explain words as well.

- Some children may need visual and non-verbal clues to support their understanding of the adult's language.

- If it is felt that some of the vocabulary is not within children's knowledge this should be explained and targeted with some direct instruction.

- New vocabulary and, in particular, new concepts may need reinforcing and being used in other ways so that the children can consolidate their new learning.

- Some children find words such as pronouns (e.g. 'he'/'it') and words that seem to have no real connection such as 'here'/'there' difficult to gain meaning from, so it is helpful if the adults use the important words (e.g. names) instead.

- Because some children take time to process information, adults should allow pauses before expecting a response. Other children may try to answer for the individual who seems to be slow and this may need to be discouraged. There needs to be a delicate balance between children being encouraged to be helpful to their peers and taking over, not allowing a particular individual a chance to act independently.

- Adults should ask children if they have any problems understanding and praise them for asking questions. To become active listeners children have to realise that they might not always understand and this is not their fault.

- Parents should be encouraged to work in the same way.

Chapter 8
Speaking activities

Once children enter school they spend less time talking and communicating within the classroom than they did in the early years settings. Children talk more at home or in play situations and as they grow older do not associate talk with active learning. In fact, teachers often want their classrooms to be quiet. It is important that children learn that speaking is a significant part of learning and it is also an important skill for later life. Therefore, children need opportunities for constructive talk as well as social talk starting from the early years. If children have articulation or speech sound problems that are not within the normal developmental limits of sound production then it might be helpful for the speech and language therapy service to be asked to carry out an assessment and provide advice.

Assessment of spoken language

Early years educators should assess children's spoken language, even if this is done informally, so that they have knowledge of children's grammatical acquisition and which language learning processes the children are able to cope with. Because expressive language is dependent upon receptive language acquisition and children cannot say words they have not learnt and internalised, it is important that adults build on the listening activities. Adults will hear when children cannot label objects correctly, when they cannot use adjectives and adverbs, when they do not have the necessary vocabulary for explanations. They have to decide whether the reserved children are quiet because this is their nature and personality or whether they are quiet because their language is not advanced enough to take part in the curriculum or social activities. There are some children who elect not to speak, 'elective mutes', and advice about their problems should be gained from speech and language therapists, paediatricians or members of the LEAs' advisory and support services. Care should be taken by adults not to feel that very talkative children are necessarily competent speakers and users of language. They may seem confident and articulate but it is only when some analysis of their spoken language takes place that it can be determined whether they have a wide range of vocabulary, a mature grammatical structure and an extensive knowledge of concepts and understanding. It is not easy to record children's speech by writing it down as they talk, as inevitably the adult misses out parts. Taping some spoken language is easier for analysis or just focusing on specific areas of speech such as using conjunctions to link sentences, coping with tenses correctly, choosing more interesting words etc. will be beneficial.

Activities to enrich expressive language

Reporting and describing

These types of talk probably make up most of the children's oral expression within the early years settings if self-maintaining and direction are discounted. This is the area of language from which learning by discovery occurs and is fundamental for children to be able to generalise and then connect ideas and concepts to each other. As in all language work, children can be encouraged to repeat what they have heard; they can be helped to generalise from one sentence to another and the adult's use of modelling, corrective feedback, is all important. The following activities are some examples:

Who am I and who are you?

Children say their names using a whole sentence (e.g. 'I'm ...' or 'My name is ...' modelled by the adult at first) and complete this with something about themselves (such as 'I am Jaswant and I can run'). The first to do this, probably the adult, then turns to the next individual and says 'Who are you?' This can take place each day at register time in order to help children to speak out in front of their peers. There are many additions to this activity and all can be about the children's own experiences (for example, their family, brothers and sisters, pets, grandparents, food preferences, toys).

What can we see?

Because children might prefer to use one-word labelling for describing, adults need to encourage them to use phrases and sentences. Brightly coloured pictures for stimuli can be provided and the children are asked what they can see in the picture. If one says 'cat' the adult will repeat 'Jenny can see a cat' or 'there is a cat on the chair' and ask for another volunteer. Although the word 'sentence' need not be introduced at first, the children can be helped to hear that several words telling about the picture can be more interesting. Describing something that has a concrete example is essential at first so that children do not have to rely on their memories. Many early years settings have a day and weather chart where pictures of the weather can be changed according to what they can see out of the window. Any activity such as this should aim for sentences to be used rather than one-word answers.

What is this?

Often young children bring in a cherished toy or something of interest from home and want to talk about it to others. Sometimes this is called 'show and tell'. Adults can help the children with questions if they seem to dry up. If some children do not bring in objects they could describe one of the classroom toys.

What did you do?

Here children do not have a picture or object stimulus and are encouraged to describe and report on common occurrences such as where they went at the weekend, what they had for breakfast, what they watched on television.

Tell it again

This needs the help of another adult who has been primed previously about the activity. To help children's auditory memories and also encourage competent and accurate reporting skills, children are sent in pairs to this other adult who either tells them something of interest or gives them a message. They have to return to the classroom and as accurately as they can report this message or item of interest to the rest of the class.

Making it more interesting

This activity helps children with using describing words. Two toys can be used as the objects and scarves are put round their necks. The sentences are 'Teddy is wearing a scarf'. 'Dumbo is wearing a scarf.' The children are encouraged to say the colour in front of 'scarf' so that the difference is shown. Any amount of adjectives and adverbs can be used in different situations. Helping children to acquire any part of speech can be given using visual clueing; for example, prepositions can be learnt through actions.

What shall I ask?

Children naturally ask questions and sometimes in the busy home or the busy early years setting these go unheeded and unanswered. If children receive negative feedback too often they might stop asking questions. Because young children require immediacy of response, they find it difficult to cope with being told to come back later. Wherever possible, if adults do not have time for an answer, they should make a quick note of the gist of the question, preferably on paper, and satisfy the child's curiosity at a later time. However, there are directed activities where children can be encouraged to ask questions. Objects or pictures can act as stimuli, especially if they are strange or out of the children's knowledge, and each individual has to think of a question to ask. Some will be simple such as 'What colour is the flower?', and others will show extension of thought such as 'Why has the train got an engine at both ends?'

Information giving

Simple reporting and describing leads on to more detailed giving of information. As children grow older they need the skill of passing on information. Most of adult expressive language is information giving, from messages concerning the school, rule consolidating and the imparting of subject area information. Once children learn to describe and tell in simple terms, they will have the structure of language needed for more detailed information giving. Children need also to have been able to express their own opinions and judgements about what they see and feel and do. They learn to make judgements and predict and begin to understand cause and effect. Using questions is important here as well as being able to answer questions logically. As children grow older they can take part in the following activities:

How does it work or what is it for?

Children bring a game or a mechanical toy from home and they have to explain what it does. Other children can be encouraged to ask questions so that the speaker has to learn how to respond. When the children can cope with explaining their own possessions they can be given something that is less known and asked to talk about it.

Come and buy

Using the home corner as a prop and turning it into a shop, pairs of children become the shopkeepers and they have to 'persuade' the other children to buy something. They can be encouraged to describe the item in glowing terms and explain why it would be useful or interesting or good to eat.

Why are they ...?

There are picture cards that can be bought showing people's faces with certain emotions or these can be pictures cut out of magazines. The children have to identify how the person might be feeling (e.g. happy, sad, cross, interested) and try to work out why they are feeling like this. There need be no rights and wrongs in this activity. A variation here can be 'what are they doing?' or 'where are they going?' In this activity children are also being helped to project or understand the feelings of others.

Answer these questions

There are two types of questions – open and closed. Often adults use more of the latter which are the ones where the answer is pre-known and there are no alternatives. Questions such as 'how old are you?' or 'what colour jumper am I wearing?' can be answered with one word and the answer will be right or wrong. Closed questions can be useful for finding out what the children have retained about some imparted information. These questions can check children's knowledge of vocabulary and whether they have been paying attention to a story. But they do not allow the children to use their own powers of imagination and prediction. The use of open questions is important for helping the children's independent thought processes.

It is within the above range of expressive language activities that children learn to verbally converse with others and to contribute thoughts and ideas to others. They have to learn to make their messages clearly understood. They have to cope with beginning and ending conversations appropriately. They have to take turns and add to the conversation, which makes what is spoken about a type of mini-discussion. As children become confident and with the aid of adults they learn to cope with what might seem quite mature language activities.

Some questions can show interest such as 'what next?', 'what if?' or 'what now?' These anticipate a thoughtful answer. Other questions allow children to make decisions and to choose for themselves such as 'shall we do ... or ...?' Others extend thought processes and require some ideas or information such as 'how does this work?' or 'what's happening?' while there are even others that extend children's curiosity such as 'what?', 'who?', 'where?' and 'why?' Conversely the questions that contain answers within them such as 'it's raining outside, isn't it?' are very limiting and no two-way conversation is demanded.

Imagining
This has been touched on in some of the activities above. It is most necessary for children to play and think imaginatively. They need to learn to play 'let's pretend'. Role-play is important here. However, children need to base their imaginative play on something they have experienced. This can come from books when they are read such stories as fairy tales and stories about animals that talk. Children believe in Father Christmas and ghosts and talking dinosaurs. As they grow older they are able to differentiate between fact and fiction. Within the early years settings children have to be allowed to be creative, to act out situations, to impersonate others (real or imaginary) and to enter the world of make-believe. Activities for this language experience are:

Let's play ...
The home corner can become anything from real-life situations such as shops, schools and hospitals to fantasy worlds such as the three bears' house, an enchanted castle or an imaginary kingdom. With the provision of costumes, children can play being in different environments and

circumstances. Left to their own devices, especially after some direct input through books and stories, they can play out different roles in different circumstances.

Let's be ...

This is as the above but with more direction from the adults. Themes are taken or particular nursery rhymes or fairy tales are used and the story lines are acted out. Often this can be turned into a performance for the parents and is the beginning of the more 'formal' plays that are seen within the school settings.

What happens when?

Nursery rhymes, fairy stories and familiar tales can have altered endings. The stories are read to the children and they are asked what might have happened if a different circumstance occurred. For example, if the woodcutter had not come along to grandmother's house when the wolf was pretending to be grandmother what might have happened to Little Red Riding Hood? Or if an ugly sister managed to wear the glass slipper would Cinderella have married the prince? There are many ways of taking this theme forward.

Let's tell a story

The adult can start a story which is as imaginative as can be and the children can be asked to say what comes next and to continue it. As this is a group activity all the children can contribute even if it is to add an adjective or adverb rather than coping with the imaginative and creative side.

Who's on the phone?

Having two old telephones (or toy telephones) can help children to pretend to talk on the phone. If two children cannot carry out a conversation together then an adult can play the part of one of the callers. If this happens the adult can determine the situation as in real life circumstances such as phoning to ask the listener to come to tea or imaginary situations where there is a crocodile in the bath and it is hungry.

Playing with puppets

Many language activities can work well through the medium of puppets. Often reserved children will cope with making their puppet talk whereas they feel too shy to talk to the class or group. Acting out situations, especially those that are make-believe, can occur with a puppet 'performance'.

Effective adults observe what the children are engaged in and take their lead from this. They understand that waiting for the children to initiate communication is of utmost importance. Waiting allows children to understand that they have control of their own learning. Bombarding children with many questions will inevitably get little or no response. If adults give children only a second or so to answer questions before providing the answers themselves, they will not allow children to become reflective. The more reflective and thoughtful children are in working out responses, the more capable they become at coping with activities throughout their school lives. Effective adults pay attention to what the children say so that an appropriate and immediate response can take place. An appropriate response is one that shows interest, one that might imitate or one that might comment. Adults as well as children have to use their powers of attention correctly.

Chapter 9
Reading activities

Reading starts with 'reading' or interpreting pictures, gaining messages from signs and symbols and it continues into learning or retaining words as whole units of meaning and then decoding unknown words into their component sounds. Children are read to by others, they share books with adults and they then learn to become independent readers. In order for competence in reading to take place, children need to have adequate abilities in receptive language understanding and expressive speech as has been emphasised in previous chapters.

Reading assessment

Children learn to read at different ages and in different developmental ways. No longer are the terms 'reading readiness' or 'pre-reading skills' used but it is still recognised that children need the foundations to be in place for the more formal skills of reading to take place later. In the early years settings there are informal assessments that can be made by adults in order to determine whether the children have the competencies necessary to make a start with the formal structure of learning reading. Simple checklists can be made in order to make it easy for the adults to determine where there might be problems. If there are difficulties with any of the tasks then direct teaching should be given.

Phonological assessment before the Reception stage

- Are the children familiar with nursery rhymes and can they recite some accurately or nearly accurately?

- Can they match pictures by their rhyme (such as pictures of hat/mat/rat/bat/cat or dog/log)?

- Can they match pictures by their initial sounds? This is alliteration using the 'onset' of the words (such as banana/baby/bicycle/bell/biscuit).

- Can they finish rhymes, usually those that are predictable (such as 'as I went through the door, I fell on the ...' or 'my mum gave me an ice, it was ever so ...')?

- Can they clap a regular beat when the adult models this?

- Can they beat syllables in familiar words (e.g. three in 'computer', two in 'table' and one in 'box')?

- Can they repeat multi-syllable words both real and nonsense (such as 'entertaining' and 'megalotious')?

Phonological assessment during the Reception year and into Year 1

- Can the children generate rhymes orally from a stimulus word (e.g. from words such as 'chair', 'door', 'sky' and 'night')?

- Can they segment words into 'onset' and 'rime' (such as 'chair' into 'ch–air' and 'pen' into 'p–en')?

- Can they blend from orally presented chunks of sound (e.g. 'ch–o–p' and 'h–ou–se')?

- Can they identify pairs of words as same or different either real words or nonsense words (auditory discrimination) using words such as 'stop/spot', 'bad/bat' or 'fun/fun'?

- Can they play 'I spy', from the adult's given initial sound or from their knowledge of initial sounds?

- Can they give the first sound (phoneme) of a given word, such as 'what sound does "cheese" begin with?' or 'what sound does "sausage" begin with?'

- Can they clap the number of syllables in any given word? (See above.)

- Can they clap a rhythm as the adult models this?

- Can they clap in time to a familiar nursery rhyme?

The *National Literacy Strategy* gives details about what phonological awareness activities can be given which then lead to work on phonics and spelling.

Assessment using books

Like the activities to help with accessing books (see below) these assessments can work during story time.

- Do the children enjoy being read to (judge by the way they attend and interact)?

- How do they listen when read to (e.g. are they quiet and attentive or are they fidgety and wanting to interrupt)?

- For how long can they concentrate?

- Do they choose to look at books (in the early years settings or at home)?

- Do they ask for books as presents (liaise with the home)?

- Do they 'pretend' to read when looking at a book (e.g. do they make up stories or retell stories)?

- Do they 'read' the pictures (see above)?

- Do they know the parts of a book such as pages, cover, pictures and details such as the title, the author and the illustrator?

- Do they show interest in the stories by asking questions or making comments?

- Do they answer questions when asked about the story? (Do they imagine what might happen next and can they explain what might be happening?) This assesses their predictive and imaginative abilities.

- Do they manage to retell common stories?

- Do they join in when a well-known story is read or when a nursery rhyme is recited?

- Can they provide a word for the end of a sentence?

- Do they seem to understand that the black marks on the page can be read? (Do they really know that the adult is 'translating' the marks on the page into words?)

- Do they understand that these marks on the page are separate words? (This is probably a skill that will not be understood by many in pre-school years.)

- Can they point to individual words? (As above, this is a skill which might be understood when words such as 'McDonalds' or 'Lego' are seen but not within a sentence or a piece of text.)

- Can they indicate that they can see the difference in the shape or length of words?

- Can they show that they can match words that are similar?

Working with books and stories

Early years settings usually have a book corner which contains comfortable chairs and/or bean bags where children can sit and look at books. It would be helpful if at least one of the larger chairs could be big enough for a child and adult to share so that interaction with books can be given in a comfortable and pleasurable manner. The books themselves should be displayed attractively so that children can browse as if in a library or bookshop. The books should look bright and cheerful, inviting the children to look at them. Wherever possible books should be replaced if they become too dog-eared. Adults in the early years settings need to accept a high turnover of books because despite all good intentions children may crack the books' spines, scribble on them without thinking, tear the pages because of fine motor control difficulties or forget to return a book.

Adults working in early years settings read stories and books to children. New books are publicised and can be 'viewed' in bookshops for potential purchase. Old favourites, of both children and adults, are often read and reread. Adults need to judge what makes a book one that will hold the children's interest and that will help them to become aware that books can be exciting, pleasurable, enjoyable and fun.

The computer and CD-ROMs also give information or help with telling stories. Children need to understand that there are different forms of books and stories.

Choosing books and stories

Adults should determine whether:

- there are a selection of bright, colourful and cheerful picture books which can be used for language development and imaginative story telling;

- the story, even if it is really simple, can be read aloud and made to sound natural and of interest;

- the language used is real and predictable;

- there is some special characteristic such as the illustrations, the use of colour, the layout and the particular content (such as humour) that will fascinate and appeal to children;

- the words and the illustrations complement each other so that the children gain correct information and interest from both;

- the story is enjoyable to both the adult and the children;

- the book can be reread without the children losing interest;

- the books are of the right length, therefore not too long;

- the words can be joined in with ease. Repetitive sentences are good for this activity as are books containing rhyme and rhythm. Poetry books are also important;

- there is a predictable and powerful story line (sometimes containing stories already known to the children);

- there are books with a strong story line and which contain stories already known to the children but are written slightly differently either using different situations, characters or approach. These are excellent for working with the children's memory skills;

- the books can be acted (can puppets be used as the characters? Can the children use 'props' to support the story?);

- wall stories can be made with the text if it is simple enough.

Activities to support early reading skills

There are many activities for helping young children to attain early reading skills that will help them to become competent readers. Looking at books and examining them when being read to can lead to young children understanding how print works.

Helping with the vocabulary of reading

Big Books are most helpful as all children, either in groups or as a whole class, can have book knowledge reinforced every time they are read to. Children are asked to interact with the book and can point in order to give answers or can handle the books in order to show what they know. Adults can ask the following:

- What is the name of this book or story?

- Where do we find the name or where does it tell us what the name is?

- Where does the story begin?

- Where is the front of the book?

- Where is the back of the book?

- Where is the first page?

- Where is the last page?

- Where is the cover?

- Where is there a picture in this book?

- Books have words in them. Where is there a word? Show me one.

- Where is the top of the page?

- Where is the bottom of the page?

- If we read along this line, where do we read next? (The adult has to model how reading works along the line from left to right and then should ask children to come and show where the words are next read when the end of the line is reached.)

Visual approaches to reading

As has been stated earlier, children learn to recall whole words from their shapes. This depends on how well they understand that the black marks on the page actually relate to an oral labelling of a word and how reliable their visual memories are. The following 'games' can be made for children in the early stages of learning whole words:

1. Matching shapes to make sure that the children have fully developed visual matching skills.

2. Classifying objects by their shape or colour or size which helps with visual discrimination.

3. Selecting one shape or picture from two overlapping pictures or from a patterned background in order to help visual discrimination (figure-ground) awareness.

4. Completing pictures of shapes and objects. Some young children may find this difficult because their fine motor skills are not sufficiently well developed. In cases such as these, they may need to talk through how they would finish the picture.

5. Looking at 'busy' pictures and picking out objects that are either readily recognisable or 'hidden' within the picture.

6. Recognising a picture as it is gradually revealed.

7. Playing dominoes with symbols or pictures (and later words). (If pictures are used in games these need to be kept simple and recognisable.)

8. Playing lotto with symbols and pictures (and later words).

9. Playing snap with symbols and pictures (and later words).

10. Using mosaics, jigsaws, pegboard activities and multi-link pictures for visual discrimination skills.

11. Finding out similarities and differences between shapes (and later words).

12. Spotting the difference on sets of three cards containing shapes where there is one with a missing detail or one with an extra detail. This can be given with picture cards or with shapes with positional changes.

13. Continuing sequences where children work out the pattern visually and then continue the sequence orally.

14. Playing 'Kim's game' in order to strengthen visual recall.

15. Matching words into their shapes (starting with children's own names).

16. Playing with and looking at different fonts so that children are not always subjected to the same 'picture' of letters.

17. Colouring, drawing and tracing which helps fine motor skills and later handwriting.

18. 'What is missing' activities so that children's visual memories are supported.

19. Visual classification activities where the adult sets the children some visual searching activities such as finding how many objects are a particular colour etc.

20. Recognising signs and symbols (e.g. those that are seen in the neighbourhood such as McDonalds).

21. Recognising objects which are altered in some way or which are drawn in silhouette.

22. Using current collection items that show how even very young children can recall and recognise pictures and names (e.g. the collecting of Pokémon cards).

From pictures and objects to words for learning

Once children can cope with games that help them discriminate, associate, match and remember using objects and pictures, they can start to recall words which is the beginning of reading. Words for first learning should be:

1. Words of personal importance such as the children's own names, words that are often seen in school or at home, words associated with pets and toys and familiar shop names which can be linked with their symbols.

2. High frequency words taken from the *National Literacy Strategy* lists. However, often these are difficult for children to recall because they cannot be visualised (e.g. how can one imagine or see a 'they' or a 'for'?).

3. Reading words with the help of a pictogram or rebus symbol that enables the children to link the spoken word with a visual clue.

4. Interesting words such as 'aeroplane', 'dinosaur' or 'elephant'. Often children can be asked what words they would like to remember.

5. Learning to recall/read simple sentences of around three to five words. These can be generated by the children. Then the words are cut out or written onto cards that the children can sequence by matching from the original and can sequence from memory. Then they can read the sentences and the individual words (in order and out of order).

6. Learning to recall/read books. Those that have repetitive sentences are easier than those that contain lots of different vocabulary.

Auditory approaches to reading

As has been stated earlier, it is important that children use sounds aurally and orally. Within the auditory approaches are those activities that help with phonological awareness, other activities that help auditory approaches over a wider area and some skills-based activities that start to enable children to learn early phonic skills. The following ideas can be used:

1. Learning to recite nursery rhymes and jingles. These should be taught as rhythmically as possible and this can be achieved by singing or acting them. Many nursery rhymes lend themselves to action, as do songs for the early years settings. As well as acting, puppets can also be used.

2. Learning playground rhymes and using these at playtimes or during PE lessons.

3. Acting out action rhymes and songs which emphasise rhythm (e.g. 'jelly on the plate').

4. Working on rhyming words. Activities such as having objects and toys that rhyme, collecting objects for a rhyming table, matching rhyming pictures, sorting pictures into rhyming sets, making up 'silly' rhymes can all be given informally to help children become aware of the similarities between words.

5. Playing 'I hear with my little ear'. This is the auditory 'I spy' and is the beginning of alliteration where children learn to connect initial sounds with actual words. Similar activities as given for rhymes can be given.

6. Thinking of words starting with a given sound before going out to play etc.

7. Learning to hear the 'odd one (sound) out'. At first this can be achieved with picture clues and later by just listening.

8. Helping a puppet 'hear' and 'say' a particular sound. The adult works the puppet and when it is shown a prop such as a cat it might say 'cap' and the children have to tell it what the word should be.

9. Becoming aware of syllables. At first the adult models by clapping syllables in children's names or nursery rhymes or songs with the children copying. Then the children can clap syllables for themselves. Percussion instruments and actions can be used to help the rhythmic nature of this activity.

10. Giving words in their component sounds for the children to blend into real words. (The adult can use strange voices to make this a game.)

As children become more adept at 'playing' orally with words and sounds then either late on in their early years settings or within the Reception class they will begin to work with more 'formal' skills which involve alphabetical knowledge and phonics for reading and spelling. The alphabet can be taught both visually and auditorially. Children learn to recognise the shape of the letter and then to attach the name of the letter. They learn to form the letter by writing and then later they discover and master the fact that letters, either singly or grouped, can be given particular sounds. It is important that adults within the early years settings avoid confusing children where the alphabet is concerned. Teaching the shape of letters and their names first is preferable because these do not change (except for the written forms of some letters such as 'a' and 'g' and these will have been looked at within visual activities).

Ideas for helping alphabetical knowledge

1. Singing the alphabet song with the adult pointing to the letters. Later the children can sing and point. It is not until the children can either place plastic or wooden letters in alphabetical order, can write the alphabet themselves and can say what comes 'before ...' or 'after ...' that it can be said that they actually know alphabetical order.

2. Learning the names of the letters by using alphabet strips or published alphabet friezes or wooden and plastic letters. Children can point to letters named by the adult, can choose letters they know, can find those within their names and other words, can match upper and lower case letters as extra activities.

3. Working on alphabetical order when lining up by using their names and their first letters. They may need to match this against the alphabet frieze. Other activities can involve ordering the children's trays, books etc.

Ideas for working on early phonic activities

1. Making alphabet books using the 'usual' basic sounds of letters. Adults must be careful in these early stages not to make children feel they are wrong if they use the hard or soft sounds for 'c' and 'g'. Either is correct. Also if their particular first name starts with a letter that is combined with another to make a sound, the children must be able to use the sounds they hear. For example, Charlotte's name

starts with the shape 'c' but the children can hear the 'sh' sound (as in 'shop'). Charlie also starts with the shape 'c' but the 'ch' sound (as in 'chop') is heard. Carly starts with the same shape but this time 'k' is heard. When alphabet books are being made, great care must be taken that the sound is listened for.

2. Making sound friezes, but again the children need to be stable with letter name recognition first.

3. Using big books with alliterative text so that the children can 'hear' the same sounds at the beginning of words plus they can 'see' the same letter shape.

4. Making and reading words using individual sounds with plastic or wooden letters so that children begin to see the rime pattern as well as hearing the same rhymes (e.g. 'm–a–n', 'p–a–n', 'D–a–n', 'r–a–n'). Children can experiment with words making nonsense and real words. As they become more proficient with this multi-sensory approach (seeing, hearing, speaking, making) they can start reading and writing these words.

Parents and reading

Reading is one of the skills within school about which parents can become very anxious. Because reading is an observable activity that is needed for nearly every school lesson, they have fears that their children may not gain the correct grades, levels or reading ages. Despite being encouraged to work on other language activities, many parents of children in the early years want to support their children with the intricacies of learning to read and then writing letters. Therefore, it is most important that parents are given helpful advice so that they work with the adults in the early years settings rather than muddling their child by giving mixed or incorrect messages and help. It also has to be realised that there might be some parents who, for a variety of reasons, do not want to help or feel that they are unable to help.

Children tend to compartmentalise school (or nursery and playgroup) and home. They will repeatedly undertake activities that they enjoy but they will try to avoid doing those activities that might make them feel foolish or that they think are too difficult. Children learn best in a relaxed atmosphere where they gain pleasure and success. Therefore, if reading activities take place in the home, parents must endeavour not to become impatient, angry, concerned or worried. They should not try to become teachers but should make reading activities a continuation of what the children are given in the early years settings. If there are lots of books in the home which are shared, read aloud by adults or older siblings, laughed at and discussed, these younger children learn that books are exciting, full of fun and information. Their main role models, their parents, reinforce the fact that reading is a pleasurable activity.

Links between early years settings and parents
The following could form home-school links:

- giving parents information about choosing books for their children, how their children choose books and setting up borrowing schemes for home;

- reinforcing to parents that their children will greatly benefit from sharing books, being read to and talking about stories they have enjoyed together;

- showing their children that they enjoy reading, sharing books and listening to stories;

- encouraging their children to 'pretend read' in their games;

- giving parents some ideas and tips for reading with their children, such as discussing the pictures, the characters and the story line. The same books can be read over and over again because children often have their favourite book. All efforts to join in and read by the children should be praised and when early reading books are used, parents need to keep as patient and relaxed as possible, especially when children appear not to be able to recall any words. Parents should refrain from encouraging their children to 'sound it out' unless they have been specifically been told to do so by teachers;

- when children can read for themselves, encouraging two books to be taken home, one for the child to read independently and one that can be read to the child by the adult;

- reminding parents that questioning is most useful, both open and closed, so that the children are helped to become curious, and that talking is as important as reading. Children and parents should exchange views and ideas and parents need to listen to what their children have to say. Some children need extra time to respond;

- reminding parents that reading should be pleasurable and enjoyable and should occur away from distractions and the television;

- discussing the merits of taped stories and videos of certain books that can be used at home. Parents may need to be reminded that it is more beneficial for their children if they watch videos with their children so that meaningful discussion and questions can take place;

- where possible, setting up reading sessions before school using books in the settings so that parents can read to their children. Where children never have a parent undertaking this activity it would be helpful for other adults to be asked to do this;

- letting parents come in after the session to borrow books;

- if possible, setting up 'reading adults' who come in to share books with groups of children. These can be parents, members of the family or helpful volunteers. Here some inservice (training) help may have to be given;

- having a book noticeboard or book tree where best buys are discussed etc.;

- making the reading diary interesting when this becomes part of the home-school links, maybe in the Reception class. Parents need to discuss the types of comments the school would find helpful;

- having a theme with a book of the day or a book of the week which is shared with parents so that they might be able to read books with the same subject with their children (or even to be able to discuss the theme);

- giving the message that when parents read with their children, both parties enjoy the sessions and that these should neither be too short nor too long;

- encouraging parents to read incidentally with their children (such as words on food packets, shop and road names, title of the video boxes);

- explaining that playing word games and listening games are also an important part of the reading process.

Children benefit from home-reading schemes whether these are formally set up or informal because they value that they have their parents' undivided attention (and it must be realised that sometimes with younger siblings this is not always possible). Children also benefit from any improvements that might be forged in the home-setting or home-school relationship and in the parent-child relationship. Home-reading can lead to later success for the children in becoming more competent readers and their increased enjoyment of books cannot be over emphasised. Working with parents with books also increases children's self-confidence and positive attitude to school which it is hoped will form the building bricks for later school life.

Chapter 10
Writing activities

Writing is probably the most difficult of the four aspects of language acquisition. It requires competent fine motor skills as most written work is formed by using either a pen or pencil. However, some writing can take place using computers. Also, occasionally, the motor skill can be taken away if children are able to compose by dictating to an adult. Writing also requires a facility in using expressive language because much that is written requires the composer to produce sentences which combine to give information of some kind, either descriptions, acquired knowledge or imaginative stories. For these a wide knowledge of word usage is needed. Sometimes writing requires one word answers or lists and sometimes more specialised types such as poetry. To get the message across and to be communicable there are conventions to be followed where punctuation is concerned and finally, what for many children can be the most difficult task, there is the requirement for words to be spelt correctly. Of course, for young children much of the above will not be attempted in the early years settings but what is learnt will form the basis of later written competencies.

Writing assessment

The two main strands to writing are composing and performing and in the very early stages these can be assessed through observing what the children can do. Some of this knowledge and some of these skills will not be seen until school entry.

Composing

- Can the children understand that spoken language can be communicated visually (e.g. that writing brings a message, that they possess the concept of 'word')?

- Do the children understand that a written message is made from words?

- Do they realise that the words are made from letters that are put in a particular order?

Performing

- Can the children tell the difference between writing and drawing?

- Can they control a writing implement? (At first children grip their pencils or crayons fistily and use the whole hand for scribbling but later start to hold the writing implement in a better pincer-type grip.)

- Can they write (make marks) from left to right across the paper? (Some children who learn letter shapes may leave spaces indicating that they understand the conventions of words on the page.)

- Can they write (make marks) from the top of the page downwards or do they scribble or mark at random?

- Do they produce some letter-like shapes and maybe some actual letters?

- Do they recognise some words such as their own name?

- Can they identify the initial sound in some words (alliterative work within phonological awareness)?

- Do they understand that the number of letters (symbols) that can be written is finite? (Have they an understanding and awareness of the alphabet?)

- Do they understand that the letters (symbols) that can be written can be repeated?

- Are the children able to form letters correctly and orientate them accurately (bearing in mind that in the early stages of writing children often find some letters difficult to write where directional aspects are concerned such as b/d/p, m/w, u/n)?

- Can they use letters to form words such as their own name?

- Can they control letter size?

- Do they leave spaces between words?

- Can they regulate their own writing and see where there might be errors?

- Have they made a start to spelling some words using symbols that match the sounds heard?

Working with writing

Writing in the early stages should be as authentic as possible so it is helpful to link writing activities with reading. The following gives some possible connections.

1. Labelling cupboards, drawers, coatpegs with the names of children and what might be contained in them and making sure that the children are aware of these.

2. Labelling other items in the classroom sometimes with one word and at others with phrases or sentences (such as 'the door is green') and again making sure that the children are aware of these. Change these at times to see if the children notice because it is too easy for them to treat such labels as they would wallpaper.

3. Labelling the play area so that it becomes a shop or a hospital or a café.

4. Using a day and weather chart every day so that the children learn to pick out relevant words for use (sometimes these will be attached to picture clues).

5. Writing the beginning of sentences such as 'I like ...', 'I come to school by ...' and asking for oral answers which are then written so that the children become aware of their words being transformed into print.

6. Using rebus symbols or pictures alongside words to help the children's recall.

7. Displaying names of the children and/or captions for their artwork.

8. Making posters for different activities.

9. Writing group thank-you letters, scribed by the adult and signed by the children.

10. Making notices for parents and using letters which are read to the children, again making them aware of the use of print.

11. Using the book corner for reinforcing why there is print.

Activities to help performing and composing

Because of the links with other areas of language, especially expressive language and reading, many of the activities already described in this book will be appropriate for helping writing. For example, the better prepared children are to speak in sentences using a choice of words, the better they will be able to transfer these ideas to the written form. If children have book awareness, they will understand the conventions of writing. If they have played visual memory games, they will be prepared to memorise the whole word for spelling purposes and if they have mastered the phonological activities, they will be able to start transferring the sounds they hear within words into letters when attempting to spell unknown words.

Helping with performing – hand-eye control and writing skills

Many of the art activities are forerunners to writing when children start experimenting with painting, drawing and early writing. Young children often experiment with both hands and it can take time for them to choose and use their preferred hand. Adults should not try to force a particular hand and should wait until the children have decided for themselves. The following activities and ideas can be of help.

1. Providing finger painting so that the children have direct control of paint on the page.

2. Providing activities such as drawing in sand so that shapes and forms can be copied and then erased.

3. Presenting some sensory activities such as 'feely bags' where the children have to feel the object in order to label it rather than seeing it, or asking the children to close their eyes and feel a particular object and then to match it from a selection of other objects or draw the object.

4. Making sure that crayons and pencils used for 'scribble' writing are not too thick for the children's small hands. When children start scribbling they clutch their crayons etc. in a fisty grip so large crayons or felt-tip pens are suitable but when they need to exercise more control they need sizes that fit more easily between their fingers.

5. Encouraging writing tasks where children scribble-write messages and 'pretend' to be writers.

6. Providing opportunities for colouring, drawing round templates, tracing and copying shapes. Joining dotted lines and drawing lines between lines help pencil control. There are many published workbooks that give such activities. It is helpful if children have left-right activities to follow as this is the direction of later writing.

7. Learning to write letters in the air by copying the adult as a model (the adult must remember to stand with his or her back to the children so another adult needs to be on hand to watch their efforts), copying letters with finger painting, in sand or flour etc. Larger movements are easier to cope with. There are books that show letter order in degrees of difficulty which can be used. There is also the debate about young children learning cursive writing or print and this is something early years settings should decide upon for themselves. Parents need to be informed and wherever possible they should be encouraged not to teach their children to write their first names in upper case letters which have to be relearnt later.

Helping with spelling

Activities that help with 'pre-spelling' overlap with those for reading and involve:

1. Orally using rhyme.

2. Working on rhyming sets.

3. Developing auditory memory skills.

4. Helping visual discrimination.

5. Increasing visual memory skills.

Once children are ready to cope with inventing spellings and learning spellings, they may be working within the demands of the *National Literacy Strategy*. This suggests that Reception aged children should be able to spell their own names and to write labels or captions for pictures and drawings and to write sentences for pictures they have drawn. It is hoped that children of this age will experiment with their writing and see how their attempt matches against or differs from the conventional spelling. In word level work they should be learning about phonemic spelling patterns. The activities to help here can include:

1. Learning important words by visual memory methods so that the whole word can be written with letters in the correct order. Such words can be high interest, like their names, family names (e.g. 'mummy', 'daddy', their siblings' or pets' names). Young children can be encouraged to look at words written on cards and to try to remember the letter order. Thus it is so important that they have alphabetical awareness. The card is turned over and the children try to reproduce the word from memory. It is better that they write or arrange plastic or wooden letters for this activity but if they say what they see this should always be by using the alphabetical names not the sounds.

2. Fitting words into shapes or outlines.

3. Looking at similarities and differences between words such as children's names (how many names have a particular letter in them or number of letters in them?) or words commonly found on food labels, shops etc.

4. Being given a word or a letter pattern and then finding this in other words.

5. Working on all the oral phonological activities and fitting sounds to written symbols. The adult has to make sure that children become aware that different letters or different combinations of letters can make the same sound.

6. Encouraging children to write using their own invented spellings and discussing these attempts. The adult can model the sentence by writing underneath and can help the children to compare the two. Children need to be praised even if their tries bear no similarity to the correct spelling, otherwise they may be disheartened.

Helping with composing

At first children's own attempts at communicating, despite seemingly random scribbling, can be 'read' by the composer. Once children become more aware of the conventions of writing and of books and print, they appear to understand that they cannot 'read' the marks they have made on the page. Although they may appear to be fluent orally their first recognisable words or part words will be limited to labels, often only one or two words. This is because they understand that as yet they find it hard to perform in the written task and that this limits their composing. In the early years settings and even in the Reception classes there are limited expectations of extended writing. Oral composing is more important. However, adults can tap into the children's oral abilities and help by:

1. Scribing a dictated sentence to write under the children's pictures and reading it with them.

2. Scribing a dictated sentence as above and encouraging the children to write over the words.

3. Scribing a dictated story and reading it with them. Word processing the stories is useful and as the children grow older and more competent with reading and using computers there are programs that help with word finding and spelling and take the strain out of the performing aspect of writing.

4. Giving ideas for composing such as pictures, story sequencing cards etc.

Chapter 11
Conclusion

Children do not necessarily learn at the same rate. Not all children will be able to communicate effectively when they leave the foundation stage of education. Their language abilities may be limited and they may have made little headway with early reading and writing skills. There was no intention within this book to discuss learning difficulties and their remediation. There are other books that do so and there are teaching programmes that are intended to work on language problems. Some of these are set out in the references.

However, the majority of children will become those literate adults with fulfilling lives described by the Secretary of State for Education in 1998. Given the right early years opportunities, they will flourish. But early years educators and parents must be aware that competence in reading and writing, those skills that are more easily assessed and that can be given scores or marks or levels, requires firm listening and speaking foundations, skills that are less easily quantifiable. Teachers must know their pupils and provide them with appropriate learning situations, each building on each other. The foundation stage can provide educational opportunities that are not burdened by time and achievement constraints. In early years settings children can help to create their individual pace of learning and this can be supported and extended by those adults who work with them.

References and recommended books for reading

Bennett, J. (1985) *Learning to Read with Picture Books*. Thimble Press: Stroud.

Branston, P. & Provis, M. (1986) *Children and Parents Enjoying Reading*. Hodder and Stoughton: London.

Bryant, P. & Bradley, L. (1985) *Children's Reading Problems*. Blackwells: Oxford.

Bryant, P. & Goswami, U. (1990) *Phonological Skills and Learning to Read*. Psychology Press: Hove.

Cooper, J., Moodley, M. & Reynell, J. (1978) *Helping Language Development*. Edward Arnold: London.

Daines, B., Fleming, P. & Miller, C. (1996) *Spotlight on Special Educational Needs: Speech and Language Difficulties*. NASEN: Tamworth.

DES (1978) *Special Educational Needs* (The Warnock Report). HMSO: London.

DES (1990) *Starting with Quality*. HMSO: London.

DfE (1995) *National Curriculum for English*. DfE: London.

DfEE (1998) *The National Literacy Strategy: Framework for Teaching*. DfEE: London.

DfEE (2000) *Teaching Assistant File. Induction training for teaching assistants* (Section 6b. Literacy (Reception) Module 6.49 - 6.92) DfEE: London.

Edwards, S. (1999) *Reading for All*. David Fulton Publishers: London.

Gains, C. & Wray, D. (eds.) (1995) *Reading Issues and Directions*. NASEN/UKRA: Tamworth.

Gorman, T. & Brooks, G. (1996) *Assessing young Children's Writing*. Basic Skills Agency: London.

Hall, N. (ed.) (1989) *Writing for Reason*. Hodder and Stoughton: Sevenoaks.

Halliday, M. (1973) *Explorations in the Functions of Language*. Edward Arnold: London.

Halliday, M. (1975) *Learning How to Mean – Explorations in the Development of Language*. Edward Arnold: London.

Harris, J. (1990) *Early Language Development: Implications for Clinical and Educational Practice*. Routledge: London.

Healy, J. (1990) *Endangered Minds: Why Children Don't Think and What We Can Do About It*. Simon and Schuster: New York.

Holloway, J. (1994) *A Rainbow of Words*. NASEN: Tamworth.

Layton, L. & Deeny, K. (1996) 'Promoting Phonological Awareness in Preschool Children' in Snowling, M. & Stackhouse, J. (eds.) *Dyslexia speech and language. A Practitioner's Handbook*. Whurr: London.

McGonagle, J. (1998) *SLA Guidelines. Promoting Literacy Through the Primary School Library*. School Library Association: Swindon.

Meek, M. (1988) *How Texts Teach What Readers Learn*. Thimble Press: Stroud.

Nicholls, J., Bauers, A., Pettitt, D., Redgwell, V., Seaman, E. & Watson, G. (1989) *Beginning Writing*. Open University Press: Milton Keynes.

Partnership Papers 1–5 (1984–1985) various authors. National Children's Bureau: London.

Pugh, G. (1985) *Partnership Paper 2. Parent Involvement: What does it mean, and how do we achieve it?* National Children's Bureau: London.

QCA (1999) *Teaching speaking and listening in Key stages 1 and 2*. QCA: London.

QCA (1999) *The National Curriculum Handbook for Primary Teachers in England Key Stages 1 and 2*. QCA: London.

QCA (2000) *Curriculum guidance for the foundation stage*. QCA: London.

Reason, R. & Boote, R. (1994) *Helping children with reading and spelling*. Routledge: London and Simon and Schuster: New York.

Sage, R. (2000) *Class talk: successful learning through effective communication*. Network Educational Press: Bodmin.

Smith, A. (1998) *Accelerated Learning in Practice*. Network Educational Press: Stafford.

Smith, D. (1985) *Spelling Games and Activities*. NASEN: Tamworth.

Smith, D. (ed.) (2000) *Success in the Literacy Hour*. NASEN: Tamworth.

Smith, D., Shirley, J. & Visser, J. (1996) *Teachers and Parents Together for Reading*. NASEN: Tamworth.

Tough, J. (1976) *Listening to Children Talking*. Ward Lock Educational: London.

Tough, J. (1977) *Talking and Learning: A Guide to Fostering Communication Skills in Nursery and Infant Schools*. Ward Lock Educational: London.

Ward, S. (1992) 'The predictive validity and accuracy of a screening test for language delay and auditory perceptual disorder', *European Journal of Communication* 27.

Waterland, L. (1985) *Read With Me: An Apprenticeship Approach to Reading*. Thimble Press: Stroud.

Webster, A. & McConnell, C. (1987) *Special Needs in Ordinary Schools: Children with Speech and Language Difficulties*. Cassell: London.

Wolfendale, S. & Bryans, T. (2001) *Word Play: Language activities for young children and their parents* (new edition). NASEN: Tamworth.